THE AUSTRALIAN
Women's Weekly
country classics

wholesome and much-loved recipes from the country table

BAUER

MEDIA GROUP

CONTENTS

The oven temperatures in this book are for conventional ovens; if you have a fan-forced oven, decrease the temperature by 10-20 degrees. A measurement conversion chart appears on the back flap of this book.

BREAKFAST

eggs benedict

PREP + COOK TIME 50 MINUTES **SERVES** 4

8 eggs

4 english muffins

200g (6½ ounces) shaved leg ham

¼ cup finely chopped fresh chives

HOLLANDAISE SAUCE

1½ tablespoons white wine vinegar

1 tablespoon lemon juice

½ teaspoon black peppercorns

2 egg yolks

125g (4 ounces) unsalted butter, melted

1 tablespoon hot water

1 Make hollandaise sauce.

2 To poach eggs, half-fill a large shallow frying pan with water; bring to the boil. Break 1 egg into a cup, then slide into pan (page 112); repeat with 3 more eggs. When all eggs are in the pan, allow water to return to the boil. Cover pan, turn off heat; stand about 4 minutes or until a light film of egg white sets over yolks. Remove eggs, one at a time, with a slotted spoon, and drain on absorbent paper (page 112); cover to keep warm.

3 Meanwhile, split muffins in half and toast.

4 Serve muffins topped with ham, poached eggs, hollandaise sauce and chives. Season with freshly ground black pepper, if you like.

hollandaise sauce Combine vinegar, juice and peppercorns in a small saucepan; bring to the boil. Reduce heat; simmer, uncovered, until liquid is reduced by half. Strain through a fine sieve into a small heatproof bowl; cool 10 minutes. Whisk egg yolks into vinegar mixture. Set bowl over a small saucepan of simmering water; do not allow water to touch base of bowl. Whisk mixture over heat until thickened (page 112). Remove bowl from heat; gradually whisk in melted butter in a thin steady stream, whisking constantly until sauce is thick and creamy (page 112). Gradually whisk in the water. Keep sauce warm, off the heat, over a saucepan of hot water.

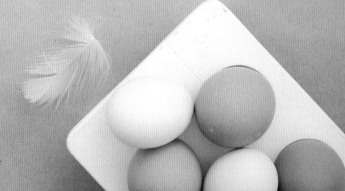

nutritional count per serving

▶ 40.6g total fat
▶ 21.2g saturated fat
▶ 2450kJ (586 cal)
▶ 24.2g carbohydrate
▶ 30.8g protein
▶ 2g fibre

cheesy leg ham and asparagus omelettes

PREP + COOK TIME 30 MINUTES   **SERVES** 4

340g (11 ounces) asparagus, trimmed

8 eggs

⅓ cup (80ml) pouring cream

2 tablespoons water

⅓ cup (25g) coarsely grated parmesan

¼ cup (30g) coarsely grated tasty cheese

2 tablespoons finely chopped fresh chives

40g (1½ ounces) butter

1 tablespoon olive oil

100g (3 ounces) sliced leg ham, cut into strips

1 Boil, steam or microwave asparagus until tender; drain.

2 Meanwhile, lightly whisk eggs, cream, the water, cheeses and half the chives in a medium bowl until combined. Season.

3 Heat a quarter of the butter and 1 teaspoon of the oil in a small frying pan over medium-high heat. When the butter is just bubbling, add a quarter of the egg mixture; tilt pan to cover base with egg mixture. Cook over medium heat until omelette is just set. Place a quarter of both the asparagus and ham on one side of the omelette. Use a spatula to lift and fold the omelette in half over asparagus and ham; cook a further 30 seconds. Carefully slide omelette onto a serving plate. Wipe out the pan.

4 Repeat with remaining butter, oil, egg mixture, asparagus and ham (wiping out the pan after each omelette), to make a total of four omelettes. Serve immediately topped with remaining chives.

nutritional count per serving
▶ 48.2g total fat
▶ 25.5g saturated fat
▶ 2247kJ (537 cal)
▶ 2.5g carbohydrate
▶ 24g protein
▶ 0.9g fibre

test kitchen tips

Using a mixture of butter
and oil stops the butter
from burning.
Don't overbeat the eggs or
the omelette will be tough.

french toast

PREP + COOK TIME 35 MINUTES   SERVES 4

250g (8 ounces) strawberries, quartered

2 tablespoons icing (confectioners') sugar

1 tablespoon water

125g (4 ounces) fresh raspberries

4 eggs

½ cup (125ml) milk

2 tablespoons caster (superfine) sugar

½ teaspoon vanilla extract

8 thick slices fruit bread (360g)

50g (1½ ounces) butter, chopped

⅔ cup (190g) Greek-style yoghurt

⅓ cup (80ml) thick (double) cream

1 Blend or process half the strawberries, half the icing sugar and all the water until smooth. Push mixture through a fine sieve into a medium bowl; discard seeds. Add raspberries and remaining strawberries to puree; mix well.

2 Whisk eggs in a medium bowl, then whisk in milk, caster sugar and extract.

3 Cut a 9cm (3½-inch) round from each slice of bread; discard crusts.

4 Heat a quarter of the butter in a medium frying pan. Dip two bread rounds into egg mixture, one at a time; cook bread rounds until browned both sides. Remove from pan; cover to keep warm. Repeat, in batches, with remaining butter, bread rounds and egg mixture.

5 Combine yoghurt and cream in a small bowl.

6 Serve french toast with yoghurt and berry mixtures; dust with remaining sifted icing sugar.

nutritional count per serving
▶ 30.7g total fat
▶ 16.8g saturated fat
▶ 2712kJ (648 cal)
▶ 71.7g carbohydrate
▶ 18.7g protein
▶ 6.8g fibre

creamy scrambled eggs

creamy scrambled eggs

PREP + COOK TIME 20 MINUTES SERVES 4

8 eggs

½ cup (125ml) pouring cream

2 tablespoons finely chopped fresh chives

30g (1 ounce) butter

4 slices wholemeal bread (180g)

1 Beat eggs, cream and chives in a medium bowl.
2 Melt butter in a large frying pan over medium heat. Add egg mixture, wait a few seconds, then use a wide spatula to gently scrape the set egg mixture from the edge of the pan to the centre (page 112); cook until egg is creamy and barely set.
3 Meanwhile, toast bread; serve toast topped with scrambled egg, season.

sunday fry-up

PREP + COOK TIME 30 MINUTES SERVES 4

50g (1½ ounces) butter

300g (9½ ounces) button mushrooms, sliced thickly

8 chipolata sausages (240g)

4 rindless bacon slices (260g)

2 medium tomatoes (190g), halved

1 tablespoon olive oil

4 eggs

1 Melt butter in a medium saucepan; cook mushrooms, stirring, for 5 minutes or until tender.
2 Meanwhile, cook sausages and bacon in a heated oiled large frying pan until bacon is crisp and sausages are cooked through. Remove from pan; cover to keep warm. Drain fat from pan.
3 Preheat grill (broiler).
4 Place tomato halves, cut-side up, onto a baking tray. Cook under grill until browned.
5 Meanwhile, heat oil in same uncleaned frying pan. Break eggs into pan; cook until egg white has set and yolk is cooked as desired.
6 Serve mushrooms, sausages, bacon, tomato and eggs with thick toast, if you like.

photograph page 12

nutritional count per serving
▶ 29.9g total fat
▶ 19.8g carbohydrate
▶ 14.5g saturated fat
▶ 20g protein
▶ 1176kJ (422 cal)
▶ 3.3g fibre

nutritional count per serving
▶ 41.3g total fat
▶ 4.4g carbohydrate
▶ 16.9g saturated fat
▶ 34g protein
▶ 2203kJ (527 cal)
▶ 3.2g fibre

sunday fry-up (recipe page 11)

blueberry bagels

PREP + COOK TIME 1¾ HOURS (+ STANDING) MAKES 12

1 cup (250ml) milk

3 teaspoons dried yeast (10g)

2 tablespoons caster (superfine) sugar

½ cup (125ml) warm water

80g (2½ ounces) frozen blueberries, thawed

3¾ cups (560g) plain (all-purpose) flour

1 teaspoon ground cinnamon

1 egg yolk

1 teaspoon water, extra

¼ cup (55g) demerara sugar

250g (8 ounces) cream cheese, softened

¼ cup (40g) icing (confectioners') sugar

125g (4 ounces) fresh blueberries

1 Heat milk until just warm. Combine yeast, half the caster sugar, the warm water and milk, and blueberries in a large bowl; whisk until yeast dissolves. Cover; stand in a warm place for about 10 minutes or until the mixture is frothy.

2 Stir sifted flour, cinnamon and remaining caster sugar into the yeast mixture; mix to a firm dough. Knead dough on a floured surface about 10 minutes or until dough is smooth and elastic. Place dough in a large oiled bowl; cover, stand in a warm place about 1 hour or until dough has doubled in size.

3 Grease two oven trays. Turn dough onto a floured surface, knead until smooth. Divide dough into 12 pieces. Shape each piece into a ball. Press a floured finger through the centre of each ball to make a hole; rotate ball with finger until the hole is a third of the size of the bagel. Place bagels about 3cm (1¼-inches) apart on trays. Cover; stand in a warm place about 15 minutes or until risen.

4 Preheat oven to 200°C/400°F.

5 Drop 3 or 4 bagels, one at a time, into a large saucepan of boiling water (don't overcrowd the pan). Turn bagels after 1 minute; boil for a further 1 minute. Remove with a slotted spoon. Return bagels to trays; brush tops with combined egg yolk and the extra water, sprinkle with demerara sugar. Bake about 20 minutes.

6 Meanwhile, beat cream cheese and sifted icing sugar in a small bowl with an electric mixer until mixture is smooth.

7 Preheat grill (broiler).

8 Split bagels; toast under hot grill. Top bagels with cream cheese mixture and fresh blueberries to serve.

nutritional count per bagel
▶ 8.8g total fat
▶ 5.2g saturated fat
▶ 1287kJ (307 cal)
▶ 47.9g carbohydrate
▶ 8.3g protein
▶ 2.3g fibre

test kitchen tip

Store bagels, split in half and wrapped in plastic wrap, in an airtight container in the freezer for up to 3 months.

test kitchen note

Developed around 1900
by Swiss physician Max
Bircher-Benner for patients
in his hospital, bircher muesli
is a popular breakfast based
on uncooked rolled oats,
fruit and nuts. We've given
this recipe a twist by serving
it with caramelised pears.

bircher muesli with caramelised poached pears

PREP + COOK TIME 50 MINUTES (+ REFRIGERATION) SERVES 6

2 cups (360g) rolled oats

1¼ cups (310ml) apple juice

1 small pear (180g)

⅓ cup (80ml) pouring cream

2 tablespoons honey

⅓ cup (95g) Greek-style yoghurt

⅓ cup (55g) sultanas (golden raisins)

⅓ cup (25g) toasted flaked almonds

⅔ cup (190g) Greek-style yoghurt, extra

CARAMELISED POACHED PEARS

8 small beurre bosc pears (1.4kg)

2 cups (500ml) dry white wine

2 cups (500ml) water

1 cup (220g) caster (superfine) sugar

½ cup (125ml) maple syrup

1 medium lemon (140g), halved

2 bay leaves

50g (1½ ounces) butter

⅓ cup (75g) firmly packed brown sugar

1 Combine oats and juice in a medium bowl. Cover; refrigerate overnight.

2 Make caramelised poached pears.

3 Coarsely grate small pear; stir grated pear, cream, honey, yoghurt, sultanas and nuts into oat mixture.

4 Serve muesli topped with caramelised poached pears and extra yoghurt.

CARAMELISED POACHED PEARS Peel and core pears; quarter lengthways. Place pears in a large saucepan with wine, the water, caster sugar, maple syrup, lemon and bay leaves; bring to the boil. Reduce heat; simmer, covered, about 30 minutes or until tender. Using a slotted spoon, remove pears from syrup (reserve syrup for another use, if you like). Cool pears slightly so they hold their shape. Melt butter in a large frying pan, add pears and brown sugar; cook, stirring occasionally, over medium heat until pears are caramelised.

tip Boil the reserved syrup until reduced by half and drizzle it over ice-cream, poached fruit, fruit muffins or cereal. We used a chardonnay-style wine to poach the pears.

nutritional count per serving
▶ 25.2g total fat
▶ 12.4g saturated fat
▶ 3261kJ (779 cal)
▶ 120.4g carbohydrate
▶ 11.5g protein
▶ 10.9g fibre

creamy honey and almond porridge

PREP + COOK TIME 25 MINUTES   SERVES 4

½ cup (40g) flaked almonds

2 tablespoons icing (confectioners') sugar

½ teaspoon ground cinnamon

2 cups (180g) rolled oats

3½ cups (875ml) milk

1 cup (250ml) pouring cream

¼ cup (90g) honey

1 Stir nuts in a small frying pan over medium heat about 2 minutes or until hot but not coloured. Add sugar and cinnamon; cook, stirring, over medium heat, about 3 minutes or until nuts are caramelised. Immediately transfer nuts to a greased oven tray; using a fork, spread into a single layer to cool.

2 Combine oats, milk, cream and 2 tablespoons of the honey in a medium saucepan over medium heat; cook, stirring, about 10 minutes or until porridge is thick and creamy. Remove from heat; stand 2 minutes.

3 Serve porridge drizzled with remaining honey; sprinkle with caramelised almonds.

nutritional count per serving
- 44.4g total fat
- 24.5g saturated fat
- 5308kJ (1268 cal)
- 64.6g carbohydrate
- 15.5g protein
- 4g fibre

test kitchen tip

We used a combination of
cherry tomatoes and baby
egg (plum) tomatoes for
this recipe.

corn and ricotta cakes with pesto and crispy bacon

PREP + COOK TIME 45 MINUTES   SERVES 4

400g (12½ ounces) mixed baby tomatoes

2 tablespoons olive oil

2 trimmed corn cobs (500g)

¾ cup (180ml) buttermilk

2 eggs, beaten lightly

½ cup (120g) ricotta

1 cup (150g) self-raising flour

2 tablespoons coarsely chopped fresh basil

8 rindless bacon slices (520g)

2 tablespoons basil pesto

2 tablespoons fresh baby basil leaves

1 Preheat oven to 200°C/400°F. Oil an oven tray.

2 Place tomatoes on oven tray; drizzle with half the oil. Bake about 15 minutes or until tomato skins start to split. Cover to keep warm.

3 Meanwhile, cut corn kernels from cobs.

4 Combine buttermilk, egg, ricotta, flour, chopped basil and corn kernels in a medium bowl; season.

5 Heat remaining oil in a large frying pan. Pour ¼-cup of corn mixture into pan (you can cook four at a time); cook about 2 minutes each side or until cooked through. Remove from pan; cover to keep warm. Repeat with remaining corn mixture.

6 Cook bacon in same heated frying pan until crisp.

7 Serve corn cakes with pesto, tomatoes and bacon; top with basil leaves.

nutritional count per serving
- ▶ 35.7g total fat
- ▶ 10.3g saturated fat
- ▶ 3066kJ (732 cal)
- ▶ 52.4g carbohydrate
- ▶ 45.6g protein
- ▶ 8.5g fibre

buttermilk pancakes with poached pears

PREP + COOK TIME 1¼ HOURS   SERVES 6

6 small pears (1kg)

2 cups (500ml) water

½ cup (110g) caster (superfine) sugar

¼ cup (90g) honey

½ medium lemon (70g), quartered

1 wide strip orange rind

½ vanilla bean

20g (¾ ounce) butter

50g (1½ ounces) butter, extra

2 cups (300g) self-raising flour

¼ cup (55g) caster (superfine) sugar, extra

2 eggs

2⅓ cups (580ml) buttermilk

cooking-oil spray

1 Peel, quarter and core pears. Place in a large saucepan with the water, sugar, honey, lemon, orange rind and vanilla bean; bring to the boil. Reduce heat; simmer, covered, 25 minutes or until pears are tender. Using a slotted spoon, remove pears from syrup. Return liquid to the boil; boil syrup until reduced to ¾ cup; discard lemon and vanilla bean. Stir in butter.

2 Meanwhile, heat extra butter until melted; cool slightly.

3 Sift flour and extra sugar into a large bowl. Gradually whisk combined eggs, buttermilk and cooled melted butter into flour mixture until smooth.

4 Spray a large heavy-based frying pan with cooking oil; pour ¼-cup of batter into heated pan (you can cook four at a time). Cook pancakes until bubbles appear on the surface; turn, brown the other side. Remove from pan; cover to keep warm. Repeat with remaining batter.

5 Serve pancakes with pears and syrup.

serving suggestion Serve the pancakes with a dollop of cinnamon cream: combine ⅔ cup thick (double) cream and 2 teaspoons cinnamon sugar in a small bowl.

nutritional count per serving
▶ 27.9g total fat
▶ 16.8g saturated fat
▶ 2921kJ (707 cal)
▶ 102g carbohydrate
▶ 12.4g protein
▶ 5.3g fibre

LUNCH

roasted vegetable fillo tart

PREP + COOK TIME 1¼ HOURS (+ COOLING) SERVES 6

6 medium egg (plum) tomatoes (450g), quartered

1 small red onion (100g), sliced thickly

2 small yellow capsicums (bell peppers) (300g), quartered

2 small red capsicums (bell peppers) (300g). quartered

100g (3 ounces) fetta cheese, crumbled

1 tablespoon finely shredded fresh basil

9 sheets fillo pastry

cooking-oil spray

1 Preheat oven to 220°C/425°F.

2 Combine tomato and onion in a medium baking dish. Roast about 30 minutes or until onion softens. Remove from oven; cool.

3 Reduce oven temperature to 200°C/400°F.

4 Meanwhile, preheat grill (broiler).

5 Roast capsicum under hot grill, skin-side up, until skin blisters and blackens; cover capsicum with plastic or paper for 5 minutes. Peel away skin, then slice capsicum thinly. Place capsicum, fetta and basil in a baking dish with tomato mixture; stir gently to combine.

6 Stack all the pastry sheets on an oiled oven tray, spraying every third sheet with cooking-oil spray. Fold all four sides of fillo stack in slightly to form a 18cm x 30cm (7¼-inch x 12-inch) tart shell. Fill shell with vegetable mixture; bake about 15 minutes.

serving suggestion Mixed green leaf salad.

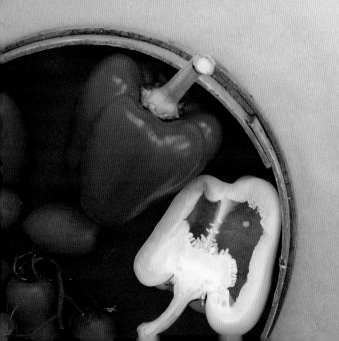

nutritional count per serving
▶ 5g total fat
▶ 2.7g saturated fat
▶ 617kJ (147 cal)
▶ 16.7g carbohydrate
▶ 7.3g protein
▶ 2.5g fibre

A firm, pale yellow, cows'-milk cheese from the Fribourg canton in Switzerland, gruyère is also produced in many regions of France. It has a sweet, nutty taste and is delicious eaten as is or used in cooking.

asparagus and gruyère tart

PREP + COOK TIME 1 HOUR (+ REFRIGERATION) **SERVES 4**

25g (¾ ounce) butter

1 small white onion (80g), sliced thinly

12 asparagus spears (225g), trimmed, halved lengthways

50g (1½ ounces) gruyère cheese, grated coarsely

2 eggs

1 teaspoon plain (all-purpose) flour

¾ cup (180ml) pouring cream

PASTRY

¾ cup (110g) plain (all-purpose) flour

75g (2½ ounces) cold butter, chopped coarsely

1 tablespoon finely grated parmesan

pinch sweet paprika

1 egg yolk

1 teaspoon iced water, approximately

1 Make pastry.

2 Preheat oven to 180°C/350°F.

3 Oil a 10cm x 34cm (4-inch x 13½-inch) loose-based fluted tart pan. Roll pastry out on a floured surface until large enough to line pan. Ease pastry into pan, press into base and sides; trim edge. Place pan on an oven tray. Refrigerate 20 minutes.

4 Line pastry with baking paper; fill with dried beans or rice (page 113). Bake 15 minutes; carefully remove paper and beans. Bake a further 10 minutes or until tart shell is browned.

5 Increase oven temperature to 200°C/400°F.

6 Meanwhile, melt butter in a large frying pan; cook onion, stirring, over low heat, for about 10 minutes or until soft.

7 Cook asparagus in a small saucepan of boiling water for 1 minute; drain. Place immediately into a bowl of iced water; drain.

8 Sprinkle onion into tart shell, top with asparagus and gruyère. Whisk eggs, flour and cream in a medium jug; pour over filling.

9 Bake tart about 20 minutes or until set.

PASTRY Process flour, butter, parmesan and paprika until crumbly. With motor operating, add egg yolk and enough of the water to make ingredients come together. Turn dough onto a floured surface; knead gently until smooth. Wrap pastry in plastic; refrigerate for 30 minutes.

nutritional count per serving
▶ 48.9g total fat
▶ 30.5g saturated fat
▶ 2445kJ (585 cal)
▶ 23.6g carbohydrate
▶ 14.2g protein
▶ 2.3g fibre

test kitchen tips

The tart shell in this recipe is 'blind baked'. This is when a pie shell or pastry case is baked before the filling is added. It is most often done if the filling is very wet, as it is in this recipe. Uncooked rice or dried beans used to weigh down the pastry are not suitable for eating. Use them every time you bake blind; cool, then store in an airtight jar.

A deep purple-red spice ground from berries grown on a Mediterranean coastal shrub, sumac adds an astringent flavour to both raw and cooked food. It suits poultry, meat and fish as well as it does a salad. Its piquancy was usually associated with Middle-Eastern foods, but these days it is used in many different cuisines.

sumac lamb and roasted vegetable sandwiches

PREP + COOK TIME 45 MINUTES   MAKES 4

¼ cup (60ml) olive oil

1 tablespoon lemon juice

1 tablespoon sumac

1 clove garlic, crushed

400g (12½ ounces) lamb backstraps

1 small eggplant (230g), sliced thinly lengthways

1 small yellow capsicum (bell pepper) (150g), sliced thickly

1 small red onion (100g), sliced thickly

2 small tomatoes (180g), sliced thickly

1 tablespoon balsamic vinegar

40g (1½ ounces) baby spinach leaves

⅓ cup loosely packed fresh flat-leaf parsley leaves

100g (3 ounces) haloumi cheese, cut into four slices

4 ciabatta rolls (400g), split

⅓ cup (80g) hummus

1 Preheat oven to 220°C/425°F.

2 Combine 1 tablespoon of the oil with the juice, sumac and garlic in a medium bowl; add lamb, turn to coat lamb in marinade.

3 Combine eggplant, capsicum, onion, tomato and vinegar with remaining oil in a large shallow baking dish. Roast about 25 minutes or until tender. Place vegetables in a medium bowl with spinach and parsley; toss gently to combine.

4 Meanwhile, cook lamb on a heated oiled barbecue grill plate (or grill or grill pan) until cooked as desired. Cover lamb; stand 5 minutes, then slice thinly.

5 Cook cheese on grill plate until browned both sides. Toast rolls on grill plate.

6 Spread hummus on four roll halves; sandwich lamb, vegetable mixture and cheese between rolls.

nutritional count per sandwich
▶ 14.7g total fat
▶ 5.5g saturated fat
▶ 2516kJ (605 cal)
▶ 82.8g carbohydrate
▶ 26.3g protein
▶ 2.6g fibre

bean salad with creamy basil dressing

PREP TIME 20 MINUTES SERVES 4

400g (12½ ounces) canned butter beans, rinsed, drained

400g (12½ ounces) canned borlotti beans, rinsed, drained

250g (8 ounces) cherry tomatoes, quartered

12 cherry bocconcini cheese (180g), halved

60g (2 ounces) baby rocket leaves (arugula)

½ cup (80g) toasted pine nuts

CREAMY BASIL DRESSING

2 tablespoons olive oil

2 tablespoons white wine vinegar

2 teaspoons white balsamic vinegar

2 tablespoons coarsely chopped fresh basil

¼ cup (60ml) pouring cream

1 Make creamy basil dressing.
2 Place salad ingredients in a large bowl with dressing; toss gently to combine.

CREAMY BASIL DRESSING Combine oil, vinegars and basil in a small bowl. Add cream; whisk until combined. Season.

nutritional count per serving
▶ 37.1g total fat
▶ 11g saturated fat
▶ 1944kJ (465 cal)
▶ 13g carbohydrate
▶ 17.1g protein
▶ 7.7g fibre

chicken schnitzel rolls with herb mayonnaise

PREP + COOK TIME 40 MINUTES MAKES 4

2 chicken breast fillets (400g), halved horizontally

2 tablespoons plain (all-purpose) flour

1 egg

1 tablespoon milk

⅔ cup (70g) packaged breadcrumbs

⅓ cup (25g) finely grated parmesan

vegetable oil, for shallow-frying

1 baby cos (romaine) lettuce (180g), leaves separated

4 slices cheddar cheese (85g)

4 ciabatta rolls (400g), cut in half

HERB MAYONNAISE

1 egg yolk

½ teaspoon table salt

1 teaspoon dijon mustard

½ cup (125ml) extra light olive oil

¼ cup (60ml) olive oil

2 teaspoons white wine vinegar

½ teaspoon finely grated lemon rind

1 tablespoon lemon juice

2 teaspoons each finely chopped fresh basil, chives and flat-leaf parsley

2 teaspoons rinsed, drained baby capers, chopped finely

1 Make herb mayonnaise.

2 Using a meat mallet, gently pound the chicken fillets, one piece at a time, between sheets of plastic wrap until 5mm (¼-inch) thick; cut each piece in half crossways.

3 Whisk flour, egg and milk in a shallow bowl; combine breadcrumbs and parmesan in another shallow bowl. Coat chicken pieces, one at a time, in egg mixture, then the breadcrumb mixture.

4 Heat oil in a large frying pan; shallow-fry chicken, in batches, until cooked through. Drain on absorbent paper.

5 Sandwich lettuce, cheddar, chicken and mayonnaise between roll halves.

HERB MAYONNAISE Combine egg yolk, salt and mustard in a medium bowl. Gradually add oils in a thin, steady stream, whisking constantly until mixture thickens. Stir in vinegar, rind, juice, herbs and capers.

nutritional count per roll
▶ 73.2g total fat
▶ 16.3g saturated fat
▶ 4558kJ (1089 cal)
▶ 61.7g carbohydrate
▶ 44.4g protein
▶ 4.6g fibre

french onion soup with gruyère croûtons

PREP + COOK TIME 1¼ HOURS SERVES 4

50g (1½ ounces) butter

4 large brown onions (800g), sliced thinly

¾ cup (180ml) dry white wine

3 cups (750ml) water

1 litre (4 cups) beef stock

1 bay leaf

1 tablespoon plain (all-purpose) flour

2 teaspoons fresh thyme leaves

GRUYÈRE CROÛTONS

1 small french bread stick (150g), cut into 2cm (¾-inch) slices

½ cup (60g) coarsely grated gruyère cheese

1 Melt butter in a large saucepan; cook onion, stirring occasionally, about 30 minutes or until caramelised.

2 Meanwhile, bring wine to the boil in a large saucepan. Stir in the water, stock and bay leaf; return to the boil. Remove from heat.

3 Stir flour into onion mixture; cook, stirring, 2 minutes. Gradually add hot stock mixture; cook, stirring, until mixture boils and thickens slightly. Reduce heat; simmer, uncovered, stirring occasionally, 20 minutes. Discard bay leaf; stir in half the thyme. Season.

4 Meanwhile, make gruyère croûtons.

5 Serve bowls of soup topped with croûtons; sprinkle with remaining thyme.

GRUYÈRE CROÛTONS Preheat grill (broiler). Toast bread on one side; turn over and sprinkle with grated cheese. Grill croûtons until cheese browns lightly.

nutritional count per serving
- 16.7g total fat
- 10g saturated fat
- 1522kJ (364 cal)
- 31.1g carbohydrate
- 13.4g protein
- 3.9g fibre

test kitchen tips

Soup can be made a day
ahead; store, covered, in
the refrigerator. Make
the croûtons just before
serving the soup.

nutritional count per serving
▶ 63.8g total fat
▶ 28.4g saturated fat
▶ 3984kJ (952 cal)
▶ 35.9g carbohydrate
▶ 57.9g protein
▶ 3.8g fibre

cream of chicken soup with parmesan cheese croûtons

PREP + COOK TIME 3 HOURS   SERVES 4

1.8kg (3½-pound) whole chicken

1 medium brown onion (150g), chopped coarsely

1 medium carrot (120g), chopped coarsely

1 stalk celery (150g), trimmed, chopped coarsely

2 litres (8 cups) water

1 litre (4 cups) chicken stock

40g (1½ ounces) butter

⅓ cup (50g) plain (all-purpose) flour

2 tablespoons lemon juice

½ cup (125ml) pouring cream

¼ cup finely chopped fresh flat-leaf parsley

PARMESAN CHEESE CROÛTONS

1 small french bread stick (150g), cut into 2cm (¾-inch) slices

½ cup (40g) coarsely grated parmesan

1 Place chicken, onion, carrot and celery in a large saucepan with the water and stock; bring to the boil. Reduce heat; simmer, covered, 1½ hours. Remove chicken from pan; simmer broth, covered, 30 minutes.

2 Strain broth through muslin-lined sieve or colander into a large heatproof bowl; discard solids.

3 Melt butter in a large saucepan, add flour; cook, stirring, until mixture bubbles and thickens. Gradually stir in broth and juice; bring to the boil. Reduce heat; simmer, uncovered, about 25 minutes or until thickened slightly. Remove from heat.

4 Discard skin and bones from chicken; shred meat coarsely. Add chicken and cream to soup; stir over heat, without boiling, until soup is heated through.

5 Meanwhile, make parmesan cheese croûtons.

6 Serve soup with croûtons; sprinkle with parsley.

PARMESAN CHEESE CROÛTONS Preheat grill (broiler). Toast bread on one side; turn over and sprinkle with grated parmesan. Grill croûtons until cheese browns lightly.

tips Soup can be made a day ahead; store, covered, in the refrigerator. Make the croûtons just before serving the soup.

quiche lorraine

PREP + COOK TIME 1½ HOURS (+ REFRIGERATION)   SERVES 6

1 medium brown onion (150g), chopped finely

3 rindless bacon slices (195g), chopped finely

3 eggs

300ml (½ pint) pouring cream

½ cup (125ml) milk

¾ cup (90g) coarsely grated gruyère cheese

PASTRY

1¾ cups (260g) plain (all-purpose) flour

150g (4½ ounces) cold butter, chopped coarsely

1 egg yolk

2 teaspoons lemon juice

⅓ cup (80ml) iced water, approximately

1 Make pastry.

2 Preheat oven to 200°C/400°F.

3 Roll pastry between sheets of baking paper until large enough to line a deep 24cm (9½-inch) round loose-based fluted tart pan. Ease pastry into pan, press into base and side; trim edge. Place pan on oven tray. Refrigerate 20 minutes.

4 Line pastry with baking paper; fill with dried beans or rice (page 113). Bake 10 minutes; carefully remove paper and beans. Bake for a further 10 minutes or until browned lightly.

5 Reduce oven temperature to 180°C/350°F.

6 Cook onion and bacon in a heated oiled small frying pan until onion is soft; drain on absorbent paper. Sprinkle bacon mixture over pastry case.

7 Whisk eggs in a large jug then whisk in cream, milk and cheese; pour into pastry case.

8 Bake quiche about 35 minutes or until set. Stand in pan 5 minutes before serving.

PASTRY Process flour and butter until crumbly. With motor operating, add egg yolk, juice and enough of the water to make ingredients come together. Turn dough onto a floured surface; knead gently until smooth. Wrap pastry in plastic; refrigerate 30 minutes.

nutritional count per serving
▶ 55.1g total fat
▶ 33.9g saturated fat
▶ 3018kJ (721 cal)
▶ 35.3g carbohydrate
▶ 21.5g protein
▶ 2g fibre

steak sandwiches with aïoli and beetroot salsa

PREP + COOK TIME 45 MINUTES   MAKES 4

1 tablespoon olive oil

1 large brown onion (200g), sliced thinly

1 tablespoon brown sugar

1 tablespoon balsamic vinegar

4 thin beef scotch fillet steaks (500g)

8 thick slices white bread (560g)

30g (1 ounce) baby rocket leaves (arugula)

2 medium tomatoes (300g), sliced thickly

AÏOLI

½ cup (150g) mayonnaise

1 clove garlic, crushed

BEETROOT SALSA

1 large beetroot (beet) (200g), peeled, grated coarsely

2 teaspoons wholegrain mustard

2 teaspoons lemon juice

2 teaspoons olive oil

1 Make aïoli and beetroot salsa.

2 Heat oil in a small frying pan; cook onion over low heat, stirring occasionally, about 10 minutes or until soft. Add sugar and vinegar; cook, stirring, about 5 minutes or until caramelised. Remove from pan.

3 Meanwhile, season steaks; cook in a heated oiled large frying pan until cooked as desired.

4 Toast bread. Sandwich rocket, tomato, steaks, onion, salsa and aïoli between toast slices.

AÏOLI Combine ingredients in a small bowl; season.

BEETROOT SALSA Combine ingredients in a medium bowl; season.

tip Beef can be cooked a day ahead. Cool; store covered, in the refrigerator.

---

nutritional count per sandwich
- ▶ 29.8g total fat
- ▶ 5.6g saturated fat
- ▶ 3202kJ (765 cal)
- ▶ 81.3g carbohydrate
- ▶ 40.8g protein
- ▶ 7.5g fibre

test kitchen tip

Aïoli is a garlic mayonnaise that originated in the south of France. Here we've used store-bought mayonnaise, rather than making it from scratch, so buy a traditional-style whole-egg mayonnaise.

TEATIME

carrot cupcakes

PREP + COOK TIME 45 MINUTES (+ COOLING) **MAKES** 18

⅓ cup (80ml) vegetable oil

½ cup (110g) firmly packed brown sugar

1 egg

1 cup firmly packed coarsely grated carrot

⅓ cup (40g) finely chopped walnuts

¾ cup (110g) self-raising flour

½ teaspoon mixed spice

1 tablespoon pepitas (dried pumpkin kernels), chopped finely

1 tablespoon finely chopped dried apricots

1 tablespoon finely chopped walnuts, extra

LEMON CREAM CHEESE FROSTING

90g (3 ounces) cream cheese, softened

30g (1 ounce) unsalted butter, softened

1 teaspoon finely grated lemon rind

1½ cups (240g) icing (confectioners') sugar

1 Preheat oven to 180°C/350°F. Line 18 holes of two 12-hole (2-tablespoon/40ml) deep flat-based patty pans with paper cases.

2 Beat oil, sugar and egg in a small bowl with an electric mixer until thick and creamy. Stir in carrot and walnuts, then sifted flour and spice. Divide mixture into paper cases.

3 Bake cakes about 20 minutes. Stand cakes in pans 5 minutes before turning, top-side up, onto a wire rack to cool.

4 Meanwhile, make lemon cream cheese frosting.

5 Spoon frosting into a piping bag fitted with a 2cm (¾-inch) fluted tube; pipe frosting onto cakes. Sprinkle cakes with combined pepitas, apricots and extra walnuts.

LEMON CREAM CHEESE FROSTING Beat cream cheese, butter and rind in a small bowl with an electric mixer until light and fluffy; gradually beat in sifted icing sugar.

storage Cakes can be stored in an airtight container, in the refrigerator, for up to 3 days. Return to room temperature before serving.

test kitchen tip

Carrots contain more sugar than most other vegetables, which adds a nice sweetness to baked cakes. You need about 2 medium carrots (240g) to get the amount of grated carrot required for this recipe.

nutritional count per cupcake
▶ 9.7g total fat
▶ 2.8g saturated fat
▶ 801kJ (191 cal)
▶ 25.2g carbohydrate
▶ 2.1g protein
▶ 0.9g fibre

Tall 850ml (8cm x 17cm) (3-inch x 6¾-inch) fruit juice cans make good nut roll tins. Use a can opener that cuts just below the rims to cut one end from the can. Wash and dry the can thoroughly before greasing well. Use a double-thickness of foil to cover the top of the can and secure with string; slash a hole in the top of the foil to allow steam to escape during baking. The nut roll tins (or fruit juice cans) need to be coated thickly with melted butter so the roll won't stick to the inside of the tin. Don't use cooking-oil spray, as this doesn't give a good enough coating and the roll will stick and be hard to turn out.

date and pecan roll

PREP + COOK TIME 1¼ HOURS SERVES 10

30g (1 ounce) unsalted butter

½ cup (125ml) water

½ cup (75g) finely chopped dried seeded dates

¼ teaspoon bicarbonate of soda (baking soda)

½ cup (110g) firmly packed brown sugar

1 cup (150g) self-raising flour

¼ cup (30g) coarsely chopped pecans

1 egg

1 Adjust oven shelves to fit an upright nut roll tin. Preheat oven to 180°C/350°F. Grease lids and the inside of a 8cm x 20cm (3-inch x 8-inch) nut roll tin evenly with melted butter; place base lid on tin, position tin upright on an oven tray.

2 Stir butter and the water in a medium saucepan over low heat until butter melts. Remove from heat; stir in dates and soda, then remaining ingredients. Spoon mixture into tin; tap tin firmly on bench to remove air pockets; position top lid.

3 Bake about 1 hour. Stand roll 5 minutes before removing lids. Shake gently to release roll onto a wire rack to cool slightly. Slice the roll and serve, warm or cold, with butter.

storage The roll can be stored in an airtight container for up to 3 days.

nutritional count per serving
▶ 5.3g total fat
▶ 2g saturated fat
▶ 684kJ (163 cal)
▶ 26.1g carbohydrate
▶ 2.6g protein
▶ 1.5g fibre

nutritional count per scone
▶ 9.2g total fat
▶ 5.8g saturated fat
▶ 803kJ (192 cal)
▶ 23.6g carbohydrate
▶ 3.1g protein
▶ 1.1g fibre

Scones are best made on the day of serving. They can be frozen for up to 3 months. Thaw in the oven, wrapped in foil, or overnight in the fridge.

date scones with whipped caramel butter

PREP + COOK TIME 40 MINUTES **MAKES** 18

30g (1 ounce) unsalted butter, softened

¼ cup (55g) brown sugar

1 egg yolk

2½ cups (375g) self-raising flour

⅓ cup (50g) finely chopped dried seeded dates

1¼ cups (310ml) buttermilk

WHIPPED CARAMEL BUTTER

150g (4½ ounces) unsalted butter, softened

¼ cup (55g) brown sugar

2 teaspoons vanilla extract

1 Preheat oven to 220°C/425°F. Grease a 22cm (9-inch) square cake pan.
2 Beat butter, sugar and egg yolk in a small bowl with an electric mixer until light and fluffy. Transfer mixture to a large bowl; add sifted flour, dates and buttermilk. Use a knife to cut the buttermilk through the flour mixture to make a soft, sticky dough. Turn dough onto a floured surface; knead gently until smooth.
3 Press dough out into a 20cm (8-inch) square, cut into nine squares using a floured knife; cut each square in half diagonally. Place scones side-by-side, just touching, in pan. Brush tops of the scones with a little extra buttermilk.
4 Bake scones about 20 minutes.
5 Meanwhile, make whipped caramel butter. Serve warm scones with whipped caramel butter.

WHIPPED CARAMEL BUTTER Beat ingredients in a small bowl with an electric mixer until light and fluffy.

caramelised apple and rhubarb pie

PREP + COOK TIME 1½ HOURS (+ REFRIGERATION, COOLING & STANDING) SERVES 8

10 medium apples (1.5kg)

80g (2½ ounces) unsalted butter, chopped

⅓ cup (75g) firmly packed brown sugar

4 cups (440g) coarsely chopped rhubarb

½ cup (110g) caster (superfine) sugar

⅓ cup (80ml) water

2 tablespoons cornflour (cornstarch)

1 egg, beaten lightly

1 tablespoon demerara sugar

PASTRY

1¾ cups (260g) plain (all-purpose) flour

½ cup (75g) self-raising flour

⅓ cup (55g) icing (confectioners') sugar

185g (6 ounces) unsalted butter, chopped

1 egg

1 tablespoon iced water, approximately

1 Peel, core and thickly slice apples. Melt butter in a large frying pan; cook apple, stirring, for about 10 minutes or until apples soften. Add brown sugar; stir until caramelised. Remove from heat; cool.

2 Meanwhile, make pastry.

3 Place rhubarb, caster sugar and half the water in a large saucepan; bring to the boil. Reduce heat; simmer, covered, about 5 minutes or until rhubarb is tender. Blend cornflour with the remaining water; stir into rhubarb mixture. Stir over heat until mixture boils and thickens. Remove from heat; fold into apple mixture. Cool 20 minutes.

4 Grease a deep round 22cm (9-inch) closed springform pan. Roll three-quarters of the pastry between sheets of baking paper until large enough to line pan. Ease pastry into pan, press into base and side; trim edge. Refrigerate 30 minutes, along with remaining pastry and any scraps.

5 Preheat oven to 200°C/400°F.

6 Spoon cold apple and rhubarb mixture into pastry case; brush edge with egg. Roll remaining pastry out into a 3mm (⅛-inch) thickness; cut into 1cm (½-inch) strips. Place strips over filling in a lattice pattern; trim ends. Brush top with remaining egg; sprinkle with demerara sugar.

7 Bake pie 20 minutes. Reduce oven temperature to 180°C/350°F; bake a further 25 minutes. Stand 15 minutes. Serve pie, warm or cold, with whipped cream, ice-cream or custard, if you like.

PASTRY Process flours, sugar and butter until crumbly. With motor operating, add egg and enough of the water to make ingredients come together. Turn dough onto a floured surface; knead gently until smooth. Enclose pastry in plastic wrap; refrigerate 30 minutes.

storage Pie can be made and stored in an airtight container, in the refrigerator, for up to 1 day.

test kitchen tip

Use either golden delicious or granny smith apples in this recipe, as they have excellent flavour and hold their shape well during baking.

nutritional count per serving
- ▶ 29.5g total fat
- ▶ 18.6g saturated fat
- ▶ 2608kJ (623 cal)
- ▶ 81.3g carbohydrate
- ▶ 7.3g protein
- ▶ 5.4g fibre

lemon and currant loaf

lemon and currant loaf

PREP + COOK TIME 1½ HOURS SERVES 10

125g (4 ounces) unsalted butter, softened

1 cup (220g) caster (superfine) sugar

2 teaspoons finely grated lemon rind

3 eggs

1 cup (150g) self-raising flour

½ cup (75g) plain (all-purpose) flour

⅓ cup (80g) sour cream, softened

2 tablespoons lemon juice

1 cup (160g) dried currants

1 Preheat oven to 180°C/350°F. Grease a 14cm x 21cm (5½-inch x 8½-inch) loaf pan; line base and long sides with baking paper, extending paper 5cm (2 inches) over sides.
2 Beat butter, sugar and rind in a small bowl with an electric mixer until light and fluffy. Beat in eggs, one at a time, until combined. Stir in sifted flours, sour cream and juice, in two batches. Stir in currants. Spread mixture into pan.
3 Bake loaf about 1 hour 10 minutes. Stand loaf in pan 10 minutes before turning, top-side up, onto a wire rack to cool.

storage Loaf can be made and stored in an airtight container for up to 3 days.

pikelets

PREP + COOK TIME 30 MINUTES MAKES 15

1 cup (150g) self-raising flour

¼ cup (55g) caster (superfine) sugar

pinch bicarbonate of soda (baking soda)

1 egg, beaten lightly

¾ cup (180ml) milk, approximately

30g (1 ounce) butter

1 Sift dry ingredients into a medium bowl. Make a well in the centre; gradually whisk in egg and enough of the milk to make a smooth batter.
2 Place 1 teaspoon of the butter in a large frying pan; swirl around pan until greased all over. Drop rounded tablespoons of batter into pan (you can cook four at a time); allow room for spreading. When bubbles begin to appear, turn pikelets; cook until browned lightly on the other side. Repeat with remaining butter and batter.
3 Serve pikelets warm, with butter or jam and cream.

storage Pikelets can be wrapped individually, or layered between pieces of plastic wrap, and frozen for up to 1 month. Thaw them at room temperature for about 20 minutes before serving.

photograph page 52

nutritional count per serving
▶ 15.2g total fat
▶ 9.2g saturated fat
▶ 1466kJ (350 cal)
▶ 49.9g carbohydrate
▶ 5g protein
▶ 1.8g fibre

nutritional count per pikelet
▶ 2.6g total fat
▶ 1.5g saturated fat
▶ 321kJ (77 cal)
▶ 11.5g carbohydrate
▶ 2g protein
▶ 0.4g fibre

pikelets (recipe page 51)

florentines (recipe page 54)

test kitchen note

Florentines, interestingly enough, do not come from Florence; in fact, their origin remains a mystery. You can substitute the peanuts with flaked almonds if you like.

florentines

PREP + COOK TIME 40 MINUTES MAKES 18

¾ cup (120g) sultanas (golden raisins)

2 cups (80g) corn flakes

¾ cup (110g) toasted unsalted peanuts, chopped coarsely

½ cup (100g) coarsely chopped red glacé cherries

⅔ cup (160ml) canned sweetened condensed milk

150g (4½ ounces) dark (semi-sweet) chocolate

1 Preheat oven to 180°C/350°F. Grease two oven trays; line with baking paper.
2 Combine sultanas, corn flakes, peanuts, cherries and condensed milk in a large bowl.
3 Drop rounded tablespoons of mixture, about 5cm (2 inches) apart, on oven trays.
4 Bake about 5 minutes; cool on trays.
5 Melt chocolate in a small heatproof bowl over a small saucepan of simmering water (don't allow water to touch base of bowl). Spread cooled florentine bases with chocolate; allow to set at room temperature.

tip For a more decorative effect, use a fork to make wavy lines.

photograph page 53

white chocolate and macadamia cookies

PREP + COOK TIME 20 MINUTES MAKES 24

1½ cups (225g) plain (all-purpose) flour

½ teaspoon bicarbonate of soda (baking soda)

¼ cup (55g) caster (superfine) sugar

⅓ cup (75g) firmly packed brown sugar

125g (4 ounces) unsalted butter, melted

½ teaspoon vanilla extract

1 egg

180g (5½ ounces) white chocolate, chopped coarsely

¾ cup (105g) roasted macadamias, chopped coarsely

1 Preheat oven to 200°C/400°F. Grease two oven trays; line with baking paper.
2 Sift flour, soda and sugars into a large bowl. Stir in butter, extract and egg, then chocolate and nuts.
3 Drop rounded tablespoons of mixture about 5cm (2 inches) apart on trays.
4 Bake cookies about 10 minutes. Cool on trays.

storage Cookies can be stored in an airtight container for up to 1 week.

---

nutritional count per florentine

► 6.2g total fat
► 2.5g saturated fat
► 693kJ (166 cal)
► 24.5g carbohydrate
► 3.3g protein
► 1g fibre

---

nutritional count per cookie

► 10.4g total fat
► 4.9g saturated fat
► 706kJ (169 cal)
► 16.4g carbohydrate
► 2.2g protein
► 0.6g fibre

white chocolate and macadamia cookies

Chelsea buns are best
made on the day of serving.
They can be frozen for up
to 3 months. Thaw in the
oven, wrapped in foil.

nutritional count per bun
▶ 15g total fat
▶ 9g saturated fat
▶ 2596kJ (620 cal)
▶ 110g carbohydrate
▶ 11.2g protein
▶ 5g fibre

chelsea buns

PREP + COOK TIME 1 HOUR (+ STANDING) **MAKES** 9

1½ cups (375ml) milk

2 x 7g (¼-ounce) sachets dry yeast

1 teaspoon caster (superfine) sugar

1 teaspoon plain (all-purpose) flour

2 cups (320g) dried currants

3 cups (750ml) water

1 teaspoon finely grated lemon rind

1 teaspoon ground cinnamon

1 egg, beaten lightly

4 cups (600g) plain (all-purpose) flour, extra

125g (4 ounces) unsalted butter

⅔ cup (150g) firmly packed brown sugar

1 tablespoon caster (superfine) sugar, extra

GLACÉ ICING

1 cup (160g) icing (confectioners') sugar

1 tablespoon milk, approximately

pink food colouring

1 Grease a deep 24cm (9½-inch) square cake pan.
2 Heat milk until just warmed. Combine yeast, caster sugar, flour and milk in a medium bowl. Cover, stand in a warm place for about 10 minutes or until mixture is frothy.
3 Meanwhile, place currants and the water in a medium saucepan; bring to the boil. Remove from heat; drain. Combine currants, rind and cinnamon in a small bowl. Whisk egg into yeast mixture.
4 Sift extra flour into a large bowl. Stir in yeast mixture; mix to a soft sticky dough. Cover; stand in a warm place about 40 minutes or until dough doubles in size.

5 Meanwhile, melt butter.
6 Turn dough onto a floured surface, knead until smooth. Roll dough into a 30cm x 40cm (12-inch x 16-inch) rectangle. Brush dough with a quarter of the butter, sprinkle with a third of the brown sugar.
7 Fold one short end two-thirds of the way up the dough; fold over top third to cover first fold (sort of like folding a business letter). Turn dough halfway around to have open end facing you.
8 Roll dough into a 30cm x 40cm (12-inch x 16-inch) rectangle. Repeat folding as before, using same amount of butter and brown sugar. Turn dough halfway round, roll into a 30cm x 40cm (12-inch x 16-inch) rectangle. Brush dough with half the remaining butter, sprinkle with remaining brown sugar and the currant mixture.
9 Preheat oven to 200°C/400°F.
10 Roll dough firmly from one of the long sides; cut evenly into 9 pieces. Place buns, cut-side up, in pan; sprinkle with extra caster sugar. Stand, uncovered, in a warm place for about 20 minutes or until buns have risen slightly.
11 Drizzle buns with remaining melted butter; bake for 5 minutes. Reduce oven temperature to 180°C/350°F; bake a further 25 minutes or until buns are golden brown.
12 Meanwhile, make glacé icing.
13 Turn buns, top-side up, onto a wire rack. Drizzle warm buns with icing.

GLACÉ ICING Sift icing sugar into a small bowl, stir in enough milk to form a thin, smooth paste; tint pink with colouring.

chocolate brownies

PREP + COOK TIME 1¼ HOURS (+ COOLING) **MAKES** 20

30g (1 ounce) unsalted butter, chopped

250g (8 ounces) dark (semi-sweet) chocolate, chopped coarsely

80g (2½ ounces) unsalted butter, extra, softened

2 teaspoons vanilla extract

1 cup (220g) firmly packed brown sugar

2 eggs

½ cup (75g) plain (all-purpose) flour

½ cup (70g) coarsely chopped roasted hazelnuts

⅓ cup (80g) sour cream, softened

CHOCOLATE ICING

125g (4 ounces) dark (semi-sweet) chocolate, chopped coarsely

60g (2 ounces) unsalted butter, chopped

1 Preheat oven to 180°C/350°F. Grease a deep 20cm (8-inch) square cake pan; line base with baking paper.
2 Melt chopped butter in a small saucepan, add chocolate; stir over low heat until chocolate is melted. Cool 5 minutes.
3 Beat softened butter, extract and sugar in a small bowl with an electric mixer until light and fluffy. Beat in eggs, one at a time, until combined. Transfer mixture to a large bowl. Stir in sifted flour, then chocolate mixture, nuts and sour cream. Spread mixture into pan.
4 Bake brownie about 45 minutes; cool in pan.
5 Make chocolate icing.
6 Turn brownie, top-side up, onto a wire rack; spread with icing. Cut into squares to serve.

CHOCOLATE ICING Melt chocolate and butter in a small heatproof bowl over a small saucepan of simmering water (do not allow water to touch the base of bowl). Remove bowl from heat; cool to room temperature. Beat with a wooden spoon until thick and spreadable.

---

nutritional count per brownie
▶ 16.1g total fat
▶ 8.8g saturated fat
▶ 1069kJ (255 cal)
▶ 25.5g carbohydrate
▶ 2.7g protein
▶ 0.7g fibre

test kitchen tip

Brownies can be stored in
an airtight container for
up to 3 days.

DINNER

lemon thyme roasted chicken

PREP + COOK TIME 1¾ HOURS (+ COOLING & STANDING) **SERVES 4**

1.8kg (3½-pound) whole chicken

40g (1½ ounces) butter

1 large brown onion (200g), chopped finely

2 cloves garlic, crushed

4 rindless bacon slices (260g), chopped finely

1 egg, beaten lightly

1½ cups (105g) stale breadcrumbs

1 tablespoon finely chopped fresh lemon thyme

80g (2½ ounces) butter, extra, softened

¼ teaspoon sea salt flakes

12 baby (dutch) carrots (840g)

1 Preheat oven to 200°C/400°F.

2 Wash chicken; pat dry inside and out with absorbent paper.

3 Melt butter in a medium frying pan; cook onion, garlic and bacon, stirring, until onion softens. Remove from heat; cool 5 minutes.

4 To make stuffing, combine bacon mixture, egg, breadcrumbs and half the thyme in a medium bowl. Fill chicken cavity with stuffing.

5 Combine extra butter and half the remaining thyme in a small bowl. Using your fingers, carefully separate the skin from the breast of the chicken; spread the thyme butter under the skin covering the breast. Secure skin over cavity with toothpicks. Tie legs together with kitchen string; tuck wings underneath. Rub remaining thyme and the salt all over the skin.

6 Place chicken in a large oiled baking dish; roast 20 minutes. Add carrots; roast a further 50 minutes or until chicken is cooked through. Stand, covered, for 10 minutes. Remove and discard toothpicks.

7 Serve chicken with carrots, and roasted potatoes and steamed sugar snap peas, if you like.

nutritional count per serving
▶ 71.9g total fat
▶ 31.3g saturated fat
▶ 4335kJ (1037 cal)
▶ 30.3g carbohydrate
▶ 65.1g protein
▶ 7.3g fibre

test kitchen tip

Soup can be made a day ahead; store, covered, in the refrigerator. Suitable to freeze for up to 1 month.

pea and ham soup

PREP + COOK TIME 2½ HOURS **SERVES** 6

1 medium brown onion (150g), chopped coarsely

2 stalks celery (300g), trimmed, chopped coarsely

2 bay leaves

1.5kg (3 pounds) ham hocks

2.5 litres (10 cups) water

1 teaspoon cracked black pepper

2 cups (400g) green split peas

1 Place onion, celery, bay leaves, ham hocks, the water and pepper in a large saucepan; bring to the boil. Reduce heat; simmer, covered, about 1½ hours. Add peas; simmer, covered, 30 minutes or until peas are tender.

2 Remove hocks from pan; when cool enough to handle, remove meat from hocks. Shred meat finely. Discard bones, fat and skin; remove and discard bay leaves.

3 Stand soup 10 minutes then blend or process half the soup mixture, in batches, until smooth. Return to pan with remaining soup mixture and ham; stir over heat until hot.

nutritional count per serving
- 12.7g total fat
- 4.6g saturated fat
- 1612kJ (385 cal)
- 32g carbohydrate
- 32.1g protein
- 7.7g fibre

When you order the pork loin, ask the butcher to leave a flap measuring about 20cm (8 inches) in length to help make rolling the stuffed loin easier.

roasted pork with cranberry sauce

PREP + COOK TIME 2 HOURS (+ STANDING) **SERVES** 8

2kg (4-pound) boneless pork loin, rind on

60g (2 ounces) butter

1 tablespoon olive oil

1 medium red onion (170g), chopped finely

1 clove garlic, crushed

90g (3 ounces) mild salami, chopped finely

1 tablespoon finely chopped fresh sage

¼ cup (35g) pistachios, toasted

¼ cup (35g) dried cranberries

½ cup (25g) fresh breadcrumbs

2 tablespoons fine table salt

½ cup (125ml) port

¼ cup (80g) cranberry sauce

1½ cups (375ml) chicken stock

1 Preheat oven to 200°C/400°F.

2 Using a sharp knife, score pork rind by making shallow cuts at 1cm (½-inch) intervals. Place pork on a board, fat-side down; slice through the thickest part of the pork horizontally, without cutting through the other side. Open pork out to form one large piece. Trim pork; reserve 150g (5 ounces) trimmings for seasoning. Blend or process remaining pork trimmings with one third of the butter.

3 Heat oil in a medium frying pan; cook onion and garlic, stirring over medium-high heat until onion softens. Add remaining butter, salami, sage, nuts and cranberries; cook, stirring, 2 minutes. Transfer mixture to a medium bowl; cool. Stir in breadcrumbs and minced pork trimmings; season.

4 Press seasoning mixture along one long side of the pork; roll pork to enclose. Tie at 2cm (¾-inch) intervals with kitchen string (page 112). Rub pork with salt; place on a wire rack in a large shallow baking dish. Roast, uncovered, about 1¼ hours or until pork is cooked through. Remove pork from dish; cover pork loosely with foil, stand 15 minutes.

5 Drain excess fat from dish, add port, sauce and stock to dish; cook, stirring, over high heat until sauce thickens slightly.

6 Serve pork with sauce, and roasted vegetables, if you like.

nutritional count per serving

▶ 36.8g total fat

▶ 14g saturated fat

▶ 2614kJ (624 cal)

▶ 13.9g carbohydrate

▶ 49.8g protein

▶ 1.2g fibre

nutritional count per serving
▶ 32.6g total fat
▶ 12.9g saturated fat
▶ 2913kJ (697 cal)
▶ 21.4g carbohydrate
▶ 69.3g protein
▶ 11g fibre

Lamb noisettes are lamb loin chops with the bone removed and the "tail" wrapped around the meaty part of the chop and secured with either kitchen string or a toothpick. Discard the toothpick before serving the lamb.

navarin of lamb

PREP + COOK TIME 2 HOURS   SERVES 4

2 tablespoons olive oil

8 lamb noisettes (800g)

1 large brown onion (200g), sliced thickly

2 cloves garlic, crushed

2 tablespoons plain (all-purpose) flour

1 cup (250ml) water

3 cups (750ml) chicken stock

½ cup (125ml) dry red wine

400g (12½ ounces) canned diced tomatoes

¼ cup (70g) tomato paste

2 dried bay leaves

2 sprigs fresh rosemary

2 stalks celery (300g), trimmed, cut into 5cm (2-inch) lengths

150g (4½ ounces) green beans, trimmed, halved

20 baby (dutch) carrots (400g), trimmed

200g (6½ ounces) button mushrooms

1 cup (120g) frozen peas

½ cup coarsely chopped fresh flat-leaf parsley

1 Heat oil in a large saucepan; cook lamb, in batches, until browned. Remove from pan.
2 Cook onion and garlic in same pan, stirring, until onion softens. Add flour; cook, stirring, until mixture bubbles and thickens. Gradually add the water, stock and wine; stir until mixture boils and thickens.
3 Return lamb to pan with tomatoes, paste, bay leaves and rosemary; bring to the boil. Reduce heat; simmer, covered, 30 minutes.
4 Add celery, beans, carrots and mushrooms to pan; simmer, covered, about 30 minutes or until vegetables are tender. Add peas; simmer, uncovered, until peas are just tender. Season to taste.
5 Remove and discard toothpicks from lamb. Serve bowls of navarin sprinkled with parsley.

serving suggestion Creamy celeriac, potato or kumara mash.

beef bourguignon pies with chips

PREP + COOK TIME 2½ HOURS   SERVES 6

12 pickling onions (480g)

6 rindless bacon slices (390g), sliced thinly

2 tablespoons olive oil

400g (12½ ounces) button mushrooms

1kg (2 pounds) gravy beef, trimmed, cut into 2cm (¾-inch) pieces

¼ cup (35g) plain (all-purpose) flour

1 tablespoon tomato paste

2 teaspoons fresh thyme leaves

1 cup (250ml) dry red wine

2 cups (500ml) beef stock

750g (1½-pound) packet frozen potato chips

2 sheets butter puff pastry

cooking-oil spray

½ cup finely chopped fresh flat-leaf parsley

1 Peel onions, leaving roots intact; halve lengthways.
2 Cook bacon in a heated large heavy-based saucepan, stirring, until crisp. Drain on absorbent paper. Cook onion, in same pan, stirring, until browned. Remove from pan.
3 Heat 2 teaspoons of the oil in the same pan; cook mushrooms, stirring, until browned. Remove from pan.
4 Coat beef in flour, shake off excess flour. Heat remaining oil in same pan; cook beef, in batches, until browned.
5 Return bacon, onion and beef to pan with tomato paste and thyme; cook, stirring, 2 minutes. Add wine and stock; bring to the boil. Reduce heat; simmer, covered, 1 hour. Add mushrooms; simmer, uncovered, a further 40 minutes or until beef is tender.
6 Meanwhile, preheat oven to 220°C/425°F. Cook chips according to directions on packet.
7 Place pastry sheets on a board; turn a 1¼-cup (310ml) ovenproof dish top-side down on pastry and cut the lid for one pie by tracing around the dish with a sharp knife. Repeat process until you have six pastry lids. Place lids on an oiled oven tray, spray with cooking-oil. Bake pastry during the last 10 minutes of chip cooking time or until lids are puffed and browned lightly.
8 Meanwhile, stir parsley into beef then divide among six 1¼-cup ovenproof dishes; top each with a pastry lid. Serve pies with chips.

nutritional count per serving
▶ 45.2g total fat
▶ 14.1g saturated fat
▶ 4393kJ (1049 cal)
▶ 85.2g carbohydrate
▶ 63.1g protein
▶ 10.3g fibre

test kitchen tip

Cassoulet can be made a day ahead; store, covered, in the refrigerator. It is also suitable to freeze, at the end of step 5, for up to 3 months.

chicken, sausage and bean cassoulet

PREP + COOK TIME 1½ HOURS   SERVES 8

1kg (2 pounds) chicken pieces

½ cup (75g) plain (all-purpose) flour

¼ cup (60ml) olive oil

10 pork chipolata sausages (300g)

1 medium brown onion (150g), chopped coarsely

1 large carrot (180g), chopped coarsely

2 cloves garlic, sliced thinly

4 sprigs fresh thyme

1 bay leaf

2 tablespoons tomato paste

800g (1½ pounds) canned diced tomatoes

1 cup (250ml) chicken stock

840g (1¾ pounds) canned white beans, rinsed, drained

1 cup (70g) stale breadcrumbs

2 tablespoons finely chopped fresh flat-leaf parsley

1 Preheat oven to 200°C/400°F.

2 Coat chicken in flour; shake off excess flour. Heat half the oil in a large flameproof casserole dish on stove top; cook chicken, in batches, until browned. Remove from dish.

3 Cook sausages in same dish until browned. Remove from dish.

4 Heat remaining oil in same dish; cook onion, carrot, garlic, thyme and bay leaf, stirring, until onion softens. Add paste; cook, stirring, 1 minute. Return chicken and sausages to dish with tomatoes and stock; bring to the boil.

5 Cover dish, transfer to oven; bake 20 minutes. Remove from oven; stir in beans. Cover; bake a further 30 minutes or until sauce thickens and chicken is tender. Season to taste.

6 Preheat grill (broiler).

7 Sprinkle cassoulet with combined breadcrumbs and parsley; place under hot grill until browned.

nutritional count per serving
▶ 26.2g total fat
▶ 7.7g saturated fat
▶ 1756kJ (420 cal)
▶ 21.6g carbohydrate
▶ 22.6g protein
▶ 5g fibre

Corned beef is a true classic that gets its name from the corn-kernel sized grains of salt that it was packed in to cure it. It is simplicity itself to cook, and serving it with a piquant sauce, like horseradish, adds bite to the sweet, gentle saltiness of the meat.

slow-cooker corned beef with horseradish sauce

PREP + COOK TIME 8½ HOURS SERVES 6

1.5kg (3-pound) piece corned silverside

1 medium brown onion (150g), chopped coarsely

1 medium carrot (120g), chopped coarsely

1 stalk celery (150g), trimmed, chopped coarsely

10 black peppercorns

1 tablespoon brown malt vinegar

1 teaspoon brown sugar

2.5 litres (10 cups) water, approximately

HORSERADISH SAUCE

2 cups (500ml) milk

45g (1½ ounces) butter

2 tablespoons plain (all-purpose) flour

1 tablespoon horseradish cream

1 tablespoon coarsely chopped fresh flat-leaf parsley

1 Rinse beef under cold water; pat dry with absorbent paper. Place beef, onion, carrot, celery, peppercorns, vinegar and sugar in a 4.5-litre (18-cup) slow cooker. Add enough of the water to barely cover beef. Cook, covered, on low, 8 hours.
2 Remove beef from cooker; discard liquid and vegetables. Cover beef to keep warm.
3 Make horseradish sauce. Serve beef with sauce.

HORSERADISH SAUCE Heat milk until hot. Melt butter in a medium saucepan, add flour; cook, stirring, 1 minute. Gradually add milk, stirring, until sauce boils and thickens. Stir in horseradish cream and parsley. Season to taste.

serving suggestion Steamed baby new (chat) potatoes and green beans.

tip The horseradish sauce is best made just before serving. However, if you make it earlier, cover the surface of the sauce with plastic wrap to stop a skin from forming. Reheat gently in a saucepan, stirring, until heated through.

nutritional count per serving
▶ 26.1g total fat
▶ 13.9g saturated fat
▶ 2266kJ (542 cal)
▶ 10.2g carbohydrate
▶ 65.7g protein
▶ 1.4g fibre

test kitchen tips

Chuck steak is a cut of beef taken from the shoulder and neck; it's an economical cut, and is great for slow-cooking, which releases its wonderful flavour. Blade steak, topside, brisket or round steak can also be used.

beef and potato casserole

PREP + COOK TIME 2¾ HOURS SERVES 6

1kg (2 pounds) beef chuck steak, cut into 2cm (¾-inch) pieces

½ cup (75g) plain (all-purpose) flour, approximately

2 tablespoons olive oil

3 small brown onions (450g), halved

2 cloves garlic, crushed

2 rindless bacon slices (130g), chopped coarsely

2 tablespoons tomato paste

3 cups (750ml) beef stock

400g (12½ ounces) canned crushed tomatoes

¼ cup (60ml) worcestershire sauce

2 medium potatoes (400g), chopped coarsely

1 medium kumara (orange sweet potato) (400g), chopped coarsely

1 large red capsicum (bell pepper) (350g), chopped coarsely

1 tablespoon fresh thyme leaves

1 Coat beef in flour, shake off excess. Heat oil in a large saucepan; cook beef, in batches, until browned. Remove from pan.

2 Cook onion, garlic and bacon in same pan, stirring, until bacon is crisp. Add paste; cook, stirring, 1 minute.

3 Return beef to pan with stock, tomatoes and sauce; bring to the boil. Reduce heat; simmer, covered, 1 hour, stirring occasionally.

4 Add potato, kumara and capsicum to pan; simmer, uncovered, stirring occasionally, about 30 minutes or until beef is tender.

5 Serve casserole sprinkled with thyme.

serving suggestion Creamy mashed potato or fresh crusty bread.

---

nutritional count per serving
▶ 21.3g total fat
▶ 5.8g saturated fat
▶ 2228kJ (532 cal)
▶ 33.7g carbohydrate
▶ 48.8g protein
▶ 4.9g fibre

Ask the butcher to remove the rind and tie the pork well. If you like, roast the salted rind on a rack, separately, in a hot oven until crackly. Serve with the pork.

braised pork with fresh sage

PREP + COOK TIME 1¾ HOURS SERVES 6

90g (3 ounces) butter, chopped coarsely

1.5kg (3 pounds) rack of pork, rind removed

2 medium carrots (240g), sliced thickly

6 baby onions (150g), peeled, left whole

4 cloves garlic, peeled, left whole

2 bay leaves

6 sprigs fresh thyme

1⅔ cups (410ml) dry white wine

⅓ cup (80ml) chicken stock

1 tablespoon fresh sage leaves

1 Preheat oven to 180°C/350°F.

2 Melt butter in a large flameproof baking dish on the stove top; cook pork until browned all over. Remove from dish.

3 Cook carrot, onions, garlic, bay leaves and thyme in same dish, stirring, until browned. Return pork to dish with 1⅓ cups of the wine. Roast, uncovered, about 1¼ hours or until cooked as desired. Remove pork from dish; cover keep warm.

4 Strain cooking liquid from dish into a small saucepan; discard vegetables. Add stock and remaining wine to pan; bring to the boil. Reduce heat; simmer 5 minutes. Stir in sage. Serve pork with sage sauce.

serving suggestion Roasted baby new (chat) potatoes and cherry truss tomatoes.

---

nutritional count per serving
- 22.5g total fat
- 11.9g saturated fat
- 1704kJ (407 cal)
- 3.4g carbohydrate
- 36.1g protein
- 1.8g fibre

test kitchen tips

We used the all-purpose sebago potato in this gratin, but you can substitute it with desiree, spunta or any good roasting potato, one that keeps its shape when cooked. Don't peel or slice the potatoes until you're ready to assemble the dish, then pat the slices dry with absorbent paper.
Veal schnitzel is thinly sliced steak available crumbed or plain (uncrumbed); we use plain schnitzel, sometimes called escalopes, in this recipe.

veal scaloppine with potato and fennel gratin

PREP + COOK TIME 1¾ HOURS SERVES 4

2 tablespoons olive oil

8 veal schnitzels (800g)

2 tablespoons lemon juice

¼ cup (60ml) dry white wine

1 clove garlic, crushed

¾ cup (180ml) chicken stock

1 teaspoon dijon mustard

2 tablespoons rinsed, drained baby capers

¼ cup coarsely chopped fresh flat-leaf parsley

POTATO AND FENNEL GRATIN

400g (12½ ounces) sebago potatoes

1 small fennel bulb (200g), sliced thinly

3 teaspoons plain (all-purpose) flour

300ml (½ pint) thickened (heavy) cream

2 tablespoons milk

20g (¾ ounce) butter

⅓ cup (25g) coarsely grated parmesan

½ cup (35g) stale breadcrumbs

1 Preheat oven to 180°C/350°F. Oil deep 1-litre (4-cup) baking dish.

2 Make potato and fennel gratin: using a sharp knife, mandolin or V-slicer, cut potatoes into very thin slices; pat dry with absorbent paper. Layer a third of the potato into dish; top with half the fennel. Continue layering remaining potato and fennel, finishing with potato.

3 Blend flour with a little cream in a medium jug; gradually stir in remaining cream and milk. Pour cream mixture over potato; dot with butter.

4 Bake gratin, covered, about 45 minutes or until vegetables are just tender. Uncover; sprinkle with combined cheese and breadcrumbs. Bake a further 20 minutes or until browned.

5 Meanwhile, heat oil in a large frying pan; cook veal, in batches, until cooked as desired. Remove from pan; cover to keep warm.

6 Add juice, wine and garlic to same pan; bring to the boil. Reduce heat; simmer, uncovered, until liquid is reduced by half. Add stock and mustard; simmer, uncovered, a further 5 minutes. Remove from heat; stir in capers and parsley.

7 Drizzle veal with sauce; serve with gratin.

---

nutritional count per serving
- ▶ 48.7g total fat
- ▶ 25.2g saturated fat
- ▶ 3114kJ (745 cal)
- ▶ 22.9g carbohydrate
- ▶ 51.7g protein
- ▶ 2.9g fibre

The best thing about cooking lamb shanks is that they require very little attention, but taste so good. You can halve the recipe to serve four.

tomato-braised lamb shanks with creamy polenta

PREP + COOK TIME 4 HOURS   SERVES 8

2 tablespoons olive oil

16 french-trimmed lamb shanks (3.2kg)

1 large red onion (300g), sliced thinly

1 clove garlic, crushed

2 tablespoons tomato paste

1 cup (250ml) dry red wine

2 cups (500ml) chicken stock

1 cup (250ml) water

400g (12½ ounces) canned diced tomatoes

2 tablespoons coarsely chopped fresh rosemary

CREAMY POLENTA

3 cups (750ml) water

2 cups (500ml) milk

1 cup (250ml) chicken stock

1½ cups (255g) polenta

½ cup (40g) coarsely grated parmesan

1 cup (250ml) pouring cream

1 Preheat oven to 200°C/400°F.

2 Heat half the oil in a large flameproof baking dish on the stove top; cook lamb, in batches, until browned. Remove from dish.

3 Heat remaining oil in same dish; cook onion and garlic, stirring, until onion softens. Add paste to pan; cook, stirring, 2 minutes. Add wine; bring to the boil. Boil, uncovered, until liquid is reduced by half.

4 Return lamb to dish with stock, the water, tomatoes and rosemary. Cover; bake in oven about 3 hours or until lamb is tender.

5 Remove lamb from dish; cover to keep warm. Reserve pan juices.

6 Meanwhile, make creamy polenta.

7 Divide polenta among serving plates; top with lamb shanks and reserved pan juices.

CREAMY POLENTA Bring the water, milk and stock to the boil in a medium saucepan; gradually stir in polenta. Cook, stirring, about 10 minutes or until polenta thickens slightly. Stir in cheese and cream. Season to taste.

nutritional count per serving
▶ 42.8g total fat
▶ 21.5g saturated fat
▶ 3113kJ (743 cal)
▶ 29.8g carbohydrate
▶ 53.9g protein
▶ 2.2g fibre

serving suggestion
Steamed sugar snap peas

nutritional count per serving
▶ 45.7g total fat
▶ 27g saturated fat
▶ 2968kJ (710 cal)
▶ 22.7g carbohydrate
▶ 40.1g protein
▶ 4.2g fibre

peppered steaks with mushroom sauce and mash

PREP + COOK TIME 30 MINUTES   SERVES 6

2 tablespoons rinsed, drained green peppercorns in brine, crushed

2 teaspoons cracked black pepper

6 x 150g (4½-ounce) beef fillet steaks

2 teaspoons olive oil

1kg (2 pounds) sebago potatoes, chopped coarsely

½ cup (125ml) milk

50g (1½ ounces) butter, chopped coarsely

40g (1½ ounces) butter, extra

400g (12½ ounces) swiss brown mushrooms, sliced thinly

½ cup (125ml) brandy

1½ cups (375ml) beef stock

300ml (½ pint) pouring cream

2 tablespoons finely chopped fresh flat-leaf parsley

1 Combine both peppers in a small bowl; press all over beef. Heat oil in a large frying pan; cook beef until cooked as desired. Remove from pan; cover to keep warm.

2 Meanwhile, boil, steam or microwave potato until tender; drain. Heat milk until hot. Mash potato in a large bowl with butter and hot milk. Season to taste; cover to keep warm.

3 Melt extra butter in the same frying pan; cook mushrooms, stirring, until tender. Add brandy; bring to the boil. Boil 5 minutes or until reduced slightly. Add stock and cream; cook, stirring, until mixture is thickened slightly. Stir in parsley.

4 Drizzle sauce over beef; serve with mash.

test kitchen tips

You can use either eye fillet or scotch fillet for the recipe. Use coarse cracked black pepper, not ground, as ground pepper will make the steaks too hot. You can make the mash well ahead of serving; it will reheat well in a microwave oven.

veal parmigiana

PREP + COOK TIME 1¾ HOURS   SERVES 4

4 veal steaks (320g)

1 egg

1 tablespoon water

⅓ cup (25g) stale breadcrumbs

¼ cup (35g) plain (all-purpose) flour

30g (1 ounce) butter

⅓ cup (80ml) olive oil

1½ cups (150g) coarsely grated mozzarella

⅓ cup (25g) finely grated parmesan

TOMATO SAUCE

1 tablespoon olive oil

1 medium brown onion (150g), chopped finely

1 stalk celery (150g), trimmed, chopped finely

1 medium red capsicum (bell pepper) (200g), chopped finely

1 clove garlic, crushed

400g (12½ ounces) canned crushed tomatoes

2 teaspoons white (granulated) sugar

1 tablespoon tomato paste

1½ cups (375ml) chicken stock

1 tablespoon each finely chopped fresh flat-leaf parsley and fresh basil

1 Make tomato sauce.
2 Using a meat mallet, gently pound veal, one piece at a time, between sheets of plastic wrap until 5mm (¼-inch) thick.
3 Whisk egg and the water in a shallow bowl. Place breadcrumbs in another shallow bowl. Coat veal pieces, one at a time, in flour; shake off excess. Dip into egg mixture, then breadcrumbs. Cover, refrigerate 10 minutes.
4 Preheat oven to 180°C/350°F.
5 Heat butter and half the oil in a large frying pan; cook veal, in batches, until browned both sides. Place veal in a large shallow ovenproof dish; top with mozzarella, tomato sauce and parmesan. Drizzle over remaining oil.
6 Bake about 20 minutes or until browned.

TOMATO SAUCE Heat oil in a medium frying pan; cook onion, celery, capsicum and garlic, stirring, until onion softens. Add tomatoes, sugar, paste and stock; bring to the boil. Reduce heat; simmer, covered, 30 minutes. Uncover; simmer until sauce thickens. Stir in herbs.

nutritional count per serving
▶ 42g total fat
▶ 14.8g saturated fat
▶ 2592kJ (620 cal)
▶ 21g carbohydrate
▶ 37g protein
▶ 3.7g fibre

serving suggestion
Green leafy salad or steamed vegetables.

nutritional count per serving
- ▶ 16.5g total fat
- ▶ 7.1g saturated fat
- ▶ 1902kJ (455 cal)
- ▶ 17.4g carbohydrate
- ▶ 45.5g protein
- ▶ 3.7g fibre

Ask the butcher for either veal or beef shin (osso buco); veal will be smaller than beef, in which case you will need about 12 pieces to serve six people. You can use a mixture of mushrooms as we have, or just one variety with a good robust flavour – you will need a total of 500g (1 pound).

slow-cooker osso buco with mixed mushrooms

PREP + COOK TIME 9 HOURS **SERVES** 6

6 large pieces beef osso buco (1.7kg)

¼ cup (35g) plain (all-purpose) flour

2 tablespoons olive oil

1 large brown onion (200g), chopped coarsely

1 cup (250ml) marsala

1½ cups (375ml) beef stock

¼ cup (60ml) worcestershire sauce

2 tablespoons wholegrain mustard

2 sprigs fresh rosemary

185g (6 ounces) swiss brown mushrooms, sliced thickly

155g (5 ounces) portobello mushrooms, cut into 8 wedges

155g (5 ounces) oyster mushrooms, chopped coarsely

½ cup (125ml) pouring cream

¼ cup (35g) gravy powder

2 tablespoons water

½ cup coarsely chopped fresh flat-leaf parsley

1 Coat beef all over in flour, shake off excess. Heat half the oil in a large frying pan; cook beef, in batches, until browned. Remove from pan.

2 Heat remaining oil in same pan; cook onion, stirring, until onion softens. Add marsala; bring to the boil. Add onion mixture to 4.5-litre (18-cup) slow cooker; stir in stock, sauce, mustard and rosemary. Place beef in cooker, fitting pieces upright and tightly packed in a single layer. Add mushrooms to cooker. Cook, covered, on low, for 8 hours.

3 Carefully remove beef from cooker; cover to keep warm. Add cream and combined gravy powder and the water to cooker; cook, covered, on high, for 10 minutes or until mixture thickens slightly. Stir in parsley; season to taste.

4 Serve beef with mushroom sauce.

serving suggestion Mashed potato or soft polenta.

chicken and tarragon pie

PREP + COOK TIME 1½ HOURS (+ REFRIGERATION) SERVES 6

1 tablespoon olive oil

1 large leek (500g), sliced thickly

2 medium carrots (240g), chopped coarsely

1 large kumara (orange sweet potato) (500g), chopped coarsely

250g (8 ounces) cauliflower, cut into small florets

1 cup (120g) frozen peas

80g (2½ ounces) butter, chopped coarsely

⅓ cup (50g) plain (all-purpose) flour

3 cups (750ml) hot chicken stock

500g (1 pound) chicken breast fillets, cut into 2cm (¾-inch) pieces

⅓ cup (80ml) thick (double) cream

2 tablespoons finely chopped fresh tarragon

1 egg yolk

2 teaspoons water

PASTRY

1⅓ cups (200g) plain (all-purpose) flour

60g (2 ounces) cold butter, chopped coarsely

60g (2 ounces) lard, chopped coarsely

2 tablespoons iced water, approximately

1 Make pastry.

2 Preheat oven to 220°C/425°F.

3 Heat oil in a large saucepan on stove top; cook leek, carrot and kumara, stirring, until leek softens. Add cauliflower and peas; cook, stirring, until cauliflower is tender. Transfer vegetable mixture to an oiled deep 2.5-litre (10-cup) ovenproof dish.

4 Melt butter in same pan; cook flour, stirring, about 2 minutes or until mixture bubbles and thickens. Gradually stir in stock; cook, stirring, until mixture boils and thickens. Reduce heat; simmer, uncovered, about 15 minutes or until reduced by half. Remove from heat; stir in chicken, cream and tarragon, season. Combine chicken mixture and vegetables in dish.

5 Roll pastry between two sheets of baking paper until slightly larger than top of dish. Cut thin strip from outside edge of pastry; press around top edge of pie dish. Place remaining pastry on top of dish; pinch edges to seal, trim excess pastry. (Cut shapes from any remaining pastry to decorate.) Brush top of pie with combined egg yolk and the water; make four small cuts in top of pastry.

6 Bake pie about 20 minutes or until browned. Stand 10 minutes before serving.

PASTRY Process flour, butter and lard until crumbly. With motor operating, add enough of the water to make ingredients come together. Turn dough onto a floured surface; knead gently until smooth. Wrap pastry in plastic wrap; refrigerate 30 minutes.

tip For information on how to wash leeks, see page 112.

test kitchen tip

Chicken pairs beautifully with other herbs, including dill, lemon grass, oregano, rosemary, sage, thyme and lemon thyme. Use any of these in place of the tarragon, if you like.

cider honey roasted lamb leg

PREP + COOK TIME 6 HOURS SERVES 6

2kg (4-pound) lamb leg

1 tablespoon olive oil

1 teaspoon sea salt flakes

2 large pears (660g), halved

1¼ cups (310ml) pear cider

¾ cup (180ml) chicken stock

6 medium potatoes (1.2kg)

2 tablespoons honey

1kg (2 pounds) baby (dutch) carrots

300g (9½ ounces) green beans

1 Preheat oven to 140°C/280°F.
2 Place lamb in a large oiled baking dish. Using a sharp knife, score skin at 2cm (¾-inch) intervals; rub surface with oil, then salt. Add pears, cider and stock to dish. Cover; roast 3 hours.

3 Remove dish from oven; add potatoes. Drizzle lamb with honey; return dish to oven. Roast, uncovered, a further 2 hours.
4 Remove lamb from dish; cover to keep warm. Remove potatoes and pears from dish; set aside. Increase oven temperature to 220°C/425°F.
5 Pour pan juices from baking dish into a medium saucepan; reserve ⅓ cup. Push pears through a fine sieve into same pan; discard solids. Bring pear mixture to the boil; boil, uncovered, about 20 minutes or until reduced by half.
6 Meanwhile, return potatoes to baking dish with carrots and reserved pan juices; roast, uncovered, about 30 minutes or until vegetables are tender.
7 Boil, steam or microwave beans until tender; drain.
8 Serve lamb with potatoes, carrots and beans, drizzle with sauce.

nutritional count per serving
▶ 23.7g total fat
▶ 10.2g saturated fat
▶ 3324kJ (794 cal)
▶ 56.7g carbohydrate
▶ 79.9g protein
▶ 10.7g fibre

CAMPFIRE

breakfast beans with bacon, sausages and eggs

PREP + COOK TIME 40 MINUTES **SERVES** 6

1 tablespoon olive oil

4 rindless bacon slices (260g), chopped coarsely

1 medium brown onion (150g), chopped coarsely

1 clove garlic, chopped coarsely

800g (1½ pounds) canned diced tomatoes

1 cup (250ml) water

¼ cup (55g) brown sugar

1 tablespoon worcestershire sauce

2 teaspoons mustard powder

800g (1½ pounds) canned butter beans, rinsed, drained

12 chipolata sausages (360g)

6 eggs

1 Heat oil in a medium camp oven; cook bacon, onion and garlic, stirring, until onion softens. Add tomatoes, the water, sugar, sauce, mustard and beans; cook, covered, about 20 minutes.
2 Meanwhile, cook sausages and eggs on oiled flat plate until sausages are cooked through and egg white has set.
3 Serve beans with sausages and eggs.

To cook using a camp oven, first light a fire using lots of wood. Dig a shallow hole into which the camp oven will fit with plenty of space around it. You need lots of glowing coals to cook in the camp oven, so make sure you burn enough wood. Remember, different woods burn at different temperatures. Using a long-handled shovel, place a bed of coals into the hole at least 7.5cm (3 inches) deep. Place the camp oven on top and then shovel more coals around the edges and over the top of the camp oven. If there is any breeze at all, then shovel some dirt around the edges of the coals too, to encourage the heat to burn in towards the camp oven. If you need to cook for longer periods of time, the top coals may need replacing with fresh ones from the camp fire. Always check for any fire bans or restrictions in the area before lighting fires. Buckets of water and piles of dirt should also be on hand for any fire emergencies.

nutritional count per serving
- ▶ 27.7g total fat
- ▶ 10.8g saturated fat
- ▶ 1865kJ (445 cal)
- ▶ 19.9g carbohydrate
- ▶ 26.8g protein
- ▶ 6.3g fibre

spicy sausage and bean stew with jacket potatoes

PREP + COOK TIME 1 HOUR **SERVES** 6

6 medium potatoes (1.2kg), unpeeled

1 tablespoon olive oil

8 thick beef sausages (1.2kg), cut into 4cm (1½-inch) pieces

2 large brown onions (400g), sliced thickly

2 cloves garlic, sliced thinly

1 teaspoon chilli flakes

700g (1½ pounds) bottled tomato pasta sauce

1¾ cups (430ml) beer

2 cups (500ml) beef stock

⅓ cup (75g) firmly packed brown sugar

400g (12½ ounces) canned borlotti beans, rinsed, drained

⅓ cup coarsely chopped fresh flat-leaf parsley

1 Wrap potatoes in two layers of foil. Place potatoes in hot coals; cook, turning occasionally, about 40 minutes or until tender.

2 Meanwhile, heat oil in a large camp oven; cook sausages, stirring, until browned. Add onion, garlic and chilli; cook, stirring, until onion softens. Add pasta sauce, beer, stock, sugar and beans; cook, covered, about 30 minutes.

3 Serve stew with potatoes; sprinkle with parsley.

tip See campfire information and safety on page 94.

---

nutritional count per serving
▶ 55.2g total fat
▶ 25g saturated fat
▶ 3922kJ (937 cal)
▶ 65.5g carbohydrate
▶ 35.3g protein
▶ 15.5g fibre

camp oven lamb roast and vegetables

camp oven lamb roast with vegetables

PREP + COOK TIME 3½ HOURS SERVES 6

2kg (4-pound) lamb leg

4 sprigs rosemary

⅓ cup (80ml) olive oil

1 litre (4 cups) chicken stock

500g (1-pound) pumpkin, unpeeled, cut into 5cm (2-inch) pieces

8 medium potatoes (1.6kg), halved

8 cloves garlic, unpeeled

2 cups (500ml) water

1 Preheat large camp oven.
2 Place lamb and rosemary in camp oven; pour oil and stock over lamb, season. Cook, covered, 1½ hours.
3 Add pumpkin, potatoes, garlic and the water to camp oven; cook, covered, a further 1½ hours or until lamb is cooked through.

tip See campfire information and safety on page 94.

nutritional count per serving	
▶ 33.4g total fat	▶ 36.8g carbohydrate
▶ 12g saturated fat	▶ 82.3g protein
▶ 3313kJ (791 cal)	▶ 5.3g fibre

beef and barley stew

PREP + COOK TIME 2½ HOURS SERVES 6

2 tablespoons olive oil

1kg (2 pounds) chuck steak, cut into 3cm (1¼-inch) pieces

2 tablespoons plain (all-purpose) flour

1 medium brown onion (150g), chopped coarsely

2 medium carrots (240g), chopped coarsely

2 stalks celery (300g), trimmed, chopped coarsely

800g (1½ pounds) canned diced tomatoes

420g (13½ ounces) canned condensed tomato soup

1.5 litres (6 cups) water

½ cup (100g) pearl barley

150g (4½ ounces) packet croûtons

1 Heat oil in a large camp oven; cook beef, stirring, until browned. Add flour, onion, carrot and celery; cook, stirring, until onion softens.
2 Add tomatoes, soup, the water and barley; cook, covered, about 2 hours or until beef is tender.
3 Serve stew topped with croûtons.

tip See campfire information and safety on page 94.

photograph page 100

nutritional count per serving	
▶ 26.7g total fat	▶ 33.7g carbohydrate
▶ 8g saturated fat	▶ 40.4g protein
▶ 2303kJ (550 cal)	▶ 6.9g fibre

beef and barley stew (recipe page 99)

100

rum and raisin damper (recipe page 102)

rum and raisin damper

PREP + COOK TIME 50 MINUTES SERVES 6

1 cup (150g) raisins

¼ cup (60ml) dark rum

2 cups (300g) self-raising flour

½ cup (110g) caster (superfine) sugar

2 tablespoons vegetable oil

1 cup (250ml) buttermilk, approximately

60g (2 ounces) butter

1 Combine raisins and rum in a small bowl.
2 Combine flour and sugar in a large bowl. Make a well in the centre, add raisin mixture, oil and enough buttermilk to mix to a soft sticky dough. Knead on a floured surface until smooth.
3 Press dough into a 15cm (6-inch) circle, place in a large greased camp oven. Cut a cross in the top of the dough about 1cm (½-inch) deep. Brush top with a little extra buttermilk; dust with a little extra flour.
4 Cook damper, covered, about 35 minutes or until damper sounds hollow when tapped.
5 Serve damper warm with butter.

tip See campfire information and safety on page 94.

photograph page 101

camp oven scones with jam and cream

PREP + COOK TIME 45 MINUTES MAKES 16

3 cups (450g) self-raising flour

1 cup (250ml) pouring cream

1 cup (250ml) lemonade, approximately

1 cup (320g) strawberry jam

300ml (½ pint) double (thick) cream

1 Place flour in a large bowl. Make a well in the centre; add pouring cream and enough lemonade to mix to a soft sticky dough. Knead gently on a floured surface until smooth.
2 Press dough out evenly to a 20cm (8-inch) square, cut 16 squares using a floured knife. Place squares, just touching, in greased camp oven.
3 Cook scones, covered, about 30 minutes or until scones sounds hollow when tapped. Serve warm scones with jam and cream.

tip See campfire information and safety on page 94.

---

nutritional count per serving
- ▶ 16g total fat
- ▶ 73.7g carbohydrate
- ▶ 6.9g saturated fat
- ▶ 7.3g protein
- ▶ 2050kJ (490 cal)
- ▶ 3.1g fibre

nutritional count per scone
- ▶ 14.1g total fat
- ▶ 35.5g carbohydrate
- ▶ 9.1g saturated fat
- ▶ 3.3g protein
- ▶ 1182kJ (282 cal)
- ▶ 1.3g fibre

test kitchen tip

These scones taste just as good served with butter and golden syrup, and a cup of tea that's been boiled in the billy over the campfire.

camp oven scones with jam and cream

PRESERVING

any berry jam

PREP + COOK TIME 40 MINUTES **MAKES** 4 CUPS

125g (4 ounces) blackberries

125g (4 ounces) blueberries

250g (8 ounces) raspberries

500g (1 pound) strawberries, hulled

⅓ cup (80ml) lemon juice

4 cups (880g) white (granulated) sugar

1 Stir ingredients in a large saucepan over high heat, without boiling, until sugar dissolves. Bring to the boil, then reduce heat; simmer, uncovered, without stirring, about 30 minutes or until jam jells when tested (page 113).

2 Pour hot jam into hot sterilised jars; seal immediately. Label and date jars when cold.

test kitchen tips

You can use any combination of berries you like to give a total weight of 1kg (2 pounds). Store jam in a cool, dark place for up to 12 months. Store open jam in the refrigerator for up to 3 months. If any mould appears on the jam, throw the jam away. For information on jelling and sterilising jars, see glossary entries '*jelling*' (page 115), and '*sterilising jars*' (page 116).

nutritional count per tablespoon
- ▶ 0g total fat
- ▶ 0g saturated fat
- ▶ 326kJ (78 cal)
- ▶ 19.5g carbohydrate
- ▶ 0.3g protein
- ▶ 0.7g fibre

This basic method of making marmalade will work with most citrus fruits including lemons, limes, grapefruit, pomelos and tangerines or various combinations of these fruits.

master orange marmalade

PREP + COOK TIME 1¾ HOURS **MAKES** 4 CUPS

1kg (2 pounds) oranges

1.5 litres (6 cups) water

4½ cups (1kg) white (granulated) sugar, approximately

1 Peel oranges, removing rind and white pith separately; slice rind thinly, reserve half the pith. Quarter oranges; slice flesh thinly, reserve any seeds. Tie reserved pith and seeds in muslin cloth.
2 Combine rind, flesh, muslin bag and the water in a large saucepan; bring to the boil. Reduce heat; simmer, covered, about 1 hour or until rind is soft. Discard muslin bag.

3 Measure fruit mixture, allow 1 cup sugar for each cup of fruit mixture. Return orange mixture and sugar to pan; stir over high heat, without boiling, until sugar dissolves. Bring to the boil; boil, uncovered, without stirring, about 30 minutes or until marmalade jells when tested (page 113).
4 Pour hot marmalade into hot sterilised jars; seal immediately. Label and date jars when cold.

nutritional count per tablespoon
▶ 0g total fat
▶ 0g saturated fat
▶ 368kJ (88 cal)
▶ 22.5g carbohydrate
▶ 0.2g protein
▶ 0.4g fibre

test kitchen tips

Marmalade can be stored in a cool, dark place for up to 12 months. Once opened, store in the refrigerator for up to 3 months. If any mould appears throw marmalade away. For information on jelling and sterilising jars, see glossary entries *'jelling'* (page 115), and *'sterilising jars'* (page 116).

test kitchen tip

Store paste in an airtight
container in the refrigerator,
for up to 12 months.

When the paste is sufficiently cooked, a wooden spoon drawn through the paste will leave a very distinct trail across the base of the pan. To dry out the paste, you can also place it in a fan-forced oven with only the fan working (no temperature set) overnight.

quince paste

PREP + COOK TIME 6 HOURS (+ COOLING) **MAKES** 5 CUPS

6 medium quinces (2.1kg)

1½ cups (375ml) water

4 cups (880g) caster (superfine) sugar

1 Peel, quarter and core quinces; tie cores in a muslin cloth. Coarsely chop quince flesh.
2 Combine quince flesh and muslin bag with the water in a large saucepan; bring to the boil. Boil, covered, about 35 minutes or until fruit is soft; discard muslin bag.
3 Strain fruit over a large heatproof bowl, reserving ½ cup of the liquid; cool 10 minutes. Blend or process fruit with reserved cooking liquid until smooth.

4 Return fruit mixture to pan with sugar; cook, stirring, over low heat, until sugar dissolves. Cook, over low heat, about 3½ hours, stirring frequently, until quince paste is very thick and deep ruby coloured.
5 Meanwhile, preheat oven to 100°C/200°F. Grease a loaf pan; line base with baking paper, extending paper 5cm (2 inches) over long sides.
6 Spread paste into pan. Bake about 1½ hours or until surface is dry to touch. Cool paste in pan. Remove from pan; wrap in baking paper, then in foil. Store in an airtight container in the refrigerator.

nutritional count per tablespoon
▶ 0g total fat
▶ 0g saturated fat
▶ 59kJ (14 cal)
▶ 17.3g carbohydrate
▶ 0.1g protein
▶ 1.3g fibre

Granny Smith apples are best for this recipe.
Store the chutney in a cool, dark place
for at least three weeks before opening.
Refrigerate after opening.

sweet fruit chutney

PREP + COOK TIME 2 HOURS   **MAKES** 9 CUPS

1kg (2 pounds) green-skinned apples

800g (1½ pounds) tomatoes, peeled, chopped coarsely

2 large brown onions (400g), chopped coarsely

1 cup (150g) coarsely chopped dried apricots

1 cup (140g) coarsely chopped seeded dried dates

1 cup (160g) dried currants

2cm (¾-inch) piece fresh ginger (10g), grated

2½ cups (625ml) brown malt vinegar

2 cups (440g) firmly packed brown sugar

2 teaspoons mixed spice

¼ teaspoon cayenne pepper

1 tablespoon coarse cooking salt (kosher salt)

1 Peel, core and coarsely chop apples. Stir ingredients in a large saucepan over high heat, without boiling, until sugar dissolves; bring to the boil. Reduce heat; simmer, uncovered, stirring occasionally, about 1½ hours or until chutney is thick.
2 Spoon hot chutney into hot sterilised jars; seal immediately. Label and date jars when cold.

tip For information on how to sterilise jars, see glossary entry 'sterilising jars' (page 116).

serving suggestion
Serve chutney with cold meats and cheese or on sandwiches.

nutritional count per tablespoon
▶ 0g total fat
▶ 0g saturated fat
▶ 138kJ (33 cal)
▶ 7.5g carbohydrate
▶ 0.3g protein
▶ 0.6g fibre

COOKING TECHNIQUES

Making hollandaise sauce (1) (page 4) Whisk the egg and vinegar mixture over a small pan of simmering water. Make sure the water doesn't touch the base of the bowl, otherwise the sauce could curdle.

Making hollandaise sauce (2) (page 4) Gradually add the melted butter in a thin steady stream, whisking all the time until the sauce is smooth and thick. If the sauce is too thick, or separates, whisk in up to 2 tablespoons of hot water until the mixture is smooth and creamy.

Poaching eggs (1) (page 4) Break one egg into a small bowl or cup and gently slide it into the simmering water; repeat with the remaining eggs. Return the water to the boil. Cover pan, turn off heat; stand until a light film of egg white sets over yolks.

Poaching eggs (2) (page 4) Use a slotted spoon to remove the eggs and drain them on absorbent paper towel. At this stage you can trim the edges of the whites if they look ragged.

Scrambling eggs (page 11) Fold the egg mixture from the edge of the pan to the centre. Remove from the heat when the eggs are still creamy and barely set.

Washing leeks removes any grit from the inside layers. Cut in half lengthwise, stopping at the root. Fan the layers out and wash under fast-running cold water.

To tie a loin of pork (page 64) Using kitchen string, tie the pork at 2cm intervals to secure the shape of the pork, and any stuffing, if using. Avoid slipping the string into the cuts in the rind.

Toasting nuts Whether it's almonds, peanuts, pistachios, or any other nut, toasting them is the same. Stir nuts over a low heat in a dry frying pan until golden brown. Remove the nuts immediately from the pan to stop them from burning.

Jelling (1) The jam is ready when two or three large drops of mixture roll along the bowl of a wooden spoon to form almost a triangle of thick jam.

Jelling (2) Drop a teaspoon of jam (left) or jelly (right) onto a chilled saucer (chill in the fridge or freezer). The jam/jelly should cool quickly to room temperature.

Jelling (3) Push the jam with your finger, the skin will wrinkle if the jam is ready. If the jam is not jelling, return it to the heat and boil it again.

To melt chocolate, place the chocolate into a heatproof bowl over a pan of barely simmering water (don't let the water touch the base of the bowl). Stir until smooth, and remove from the pan as soon as it's melted.

To blind bake (1) Blind baking is when a pastry case is baked before the filling is added. It is most often done if the filling is very wet, or if the filling needs no cooking, just setting or refrigeration. Line the pastry with baking paper; if you screw up the paper first, it will be easier to line the pastry case.

To blind bake (2) after covering the pastry with baking paper, fill it with uncooked rice or dried beans. Cook the pastry for 10 minutes, then remove the paper and rice or beans, and cook the pastry case a further 10 minutes, or until the pastry is golden. Store the beans or rice, and reuse each time you need to blind bake a pastry case.

Greasing a date roll tin Using a pastry brush, grease the nut roll tins well with very soft butter. The tin needs to be coated thickly with the butter so the roll won't stick to the inside of the tin. Don't use cooking-oil spray, as this doesn't give a good enough coating and the roll will stick and be hard to turn out. Place a round of baking paper inside the top and bottom lids.

Filling a date roll tin Before turning on the oven or filling the tins, adjust the oven shelves to fit the upright nut roll tins. Spoon the cake mixture into the tins, filling them to just above halfway. Because the nut roll tin is narrow, the mixture tends to rise quite a lot, so don't over-fill the tins.

GLOSSARY

ALMONDS
flaked paper-thin slices.
ground also known as almond meal.
vienna toffee-coated almonds.

BACON SLICES also called rashers.

BAKING PAPER (parchment paper or baking parchment) is a silicone-coated paper that is primarily used for lining baking pans and oven trays so cakes and biscuits won't stick, making removal easy.

BEANS
butter cans labelled butter beans are, in fact, cannellini beans. Confusingly, butter beans is also another name for lima beans. Is a large beige bean with a mealy texture and mild taste; sold both dried and canned.
white a generic term we use for canned or dried cannellini, great northern, navy or haricot beans, all of which can be substituted for the other.

BEEF
corned beef also called corned silverside. Cut from the upper leg and cured; has little fat. Sold cryovac-packed in brine.
chuck comes from the shoulder and neck of the beef; tends to be chewy but flavourful and inexpensive. A good cut for braising or stewing.
gravy boneless stewing beef from the shin; slow-cooked, it imbues stocks, soups and casseroles with a rich flavour. Cut crossways, with the bone in, it is known as osso buco.
osso buco see beef, gravy (above).
rib roast a roast cut from the rib section that may contain two to seven rib bones. Also known as a prime, or standing rib, roast.
scotch fillet cut from the muscle running behind the shoulder along the spine. Also known as cube roll, cuts include standing rib roast and rib-eye.
silverside also called topside roast; the actual cut used for making corned beef. Sold cryovac-packed in brine.

BICARBONATE OF SODA also known as baking, or carb, soda; a raising agent.

BREAD
ciabatta in Italian, the word means slipper, the traditional shape of this popular crisp-crusted, open-textured white sourdough bread.
english muffin a round teacake made with yeast; often confused with crumpets. Pre-baked, muffins should be split open and toasted before eating.

french bread stick bread that's been formed into a long, narrow cylindrical loaf. Also known as baguette.

BREADCRUMBS
fresh bread, usually white, processed into crumbs; good for poultry stuffings.
packaged fine-textured, crunchy, purchased white breadcrumbs.
stale one- or two-day-old bread made into crumbs by blending or processing.

BUTTER we use salted butter unless stated otherwise; 125g is equal to 1 stick (4 ounces).

BUTTERMILK originally the term given to the slightly sour liquid left after butter was churned from cream, today it is made similarly to yoghurt. Sold alongside fresh milk products in supermarkets; despite the implication of its name, it's low in fat.

CHERRIES, GLACÉ also called candied cherries; cherries are boiled in a heavy sugar syrup and then dried.

CHICKEN
breast fillet the breast is halved, boned and skinned.
thigh the skin and bone remains intact.
thigh fillet skin and bone are removed.

CHILLIES use rubber gloves when handling fresh chillies as they can burn your skin.

CHIPOLATA SAUSAGE a small, highly spiced, coarsely textured beef sausage.

CHOCOLATE
dark (semi-sweet) also called luxury chocolate; made of a high percentage of cocoa liquor and cocoa butter, and a little added sugar.
chocolate hazelnut spread also known as Nutella; made of cocoa powder, hazelnuts, sugar and milk.

CINNAMON available in pieces (called sticks or quills) or ground into powder; one of the world's most common spices.

CLOVES dried flower buds of a tropical tree; can be used whole or in ground form. they have a strong scent and taste so should be used sparingly.

COCONUT
desiccated concentrated, dried, unsweetened and finely shredded coconut flesh.
shredded unsweetened thin strips of dried coconut flesh.

CORNFLOUR (cornstarch) available made from corn (maize) or wheat; used as a thickening agent in cooking.

CRANBERRIES, DRIED have a rich, astringent flavour and can be used in sweet and savoury dishes. The dried version can usually be substituted for, or with, other dried fruit.

CREAM
pouring also known as pure or fresh cream. It has no additives and contains a minimum fat content of 35%.
sour a thick commercially-cultured soured cream. Minimum fat content 35%.
thick (double) a dolloping cream with a minimum fat content of 45%.
thickened (heavy) a whipping cream that contains a thickener. It has a minimum fat content of 35%.

CURRANTS, DRIED tiny, seedless, almost black raisins so-named after a grape variety that originated in Corinth, Greece. Not the same as fresh currants.

CUSTARD POWDER instant mixture used to make pouring custard; similar to North American instant pudding mixes.

EGGS we use large chicken eggs that weigh an average of 60g (2 ounces). If a recipe calls for raw or barely cooked eggs, exercise caution if there is a salmonella problem in your area, particularly in food eaten by children, pregnant women or the elderly or infirm.

FLOUR
plain (all-purpose) an all-purpose flour made from wheat.
self-raising all-purpose plain or wholemeal flour with baking powder added; make at home in the proportion of 1 cup plain or wholemeal flour to 2 teaspoons baking powder.

FOOD COLOURING dyes used to change the colour of various foods. These dyes can be eaten and do not change the taste to a noticeable extent.

GELATINE a thickening agent; we use powdered (dried) gelatine; it's also available in sheets known as leaf gelatine. Three teaspoons of powdered gelatine (7g or one sachet) is about the same as four leaves.

GINGER, FRESH also called green or root ginger; the thick gnarled root of a tropical plant.

HAZELNUTS also known as filberts; plump, grape-sized, rich, sweet nuts.

HONEY the variety sold in a squeezable container is not suitable for the recipes in this book as it is too runny.

HORSERADISH CREAM a commercially made creamy paste consisting of grated horseradish, vinegar, oil and sugar. Don't confuse it with prepared horseradish, which is the preserved grated root.

JELLING (testing when a jam is set) dip a wooden spoon into the jam, and hold the bowl of the spoon towards you. if the jam is ready, two or three large drops will roll along the edge of the spoon to form almost a triangle of thick jam. Drop a teaspoon of jam onto a chilled (in the fridge or freezer) saucer. The jam should cool quickly to room temperature. Push the jam with your finger, the skin will wrinkle if the jam is ready. If the jam is not jelling, return it to the heat and boil it again.

KITCHEN STRING made of a natural product such as cotton or hemp so that it neither affects the flavour of the food it's tied around nor melts when heated.

KIWIFRUIT also known as chinese gooseberry; has a brown, somewhat hairy skin and bright-green flesh with a unique sweet-tart flavour.

KUMARA (orange sweet potato) the Polynesian name of an orange-fleshed sweet potato often confused with yam; good baked, boiled, mashed or fried, similarly to other potatoes.

LAMB
backstrap also known as eye of loin; the larger fillet from the loin.
easy-carve leg lamb leg with all but the shank bone removed for faster roasting and stress-free carving.
leg cut from the hindquarter; can be boned, butterflied, rolled and tied, or diced into cubes.

LARD the rendered fat of a pig, used in cooking and baking.

MAPLE SYRUP distilled from the sap of sugar maple trees. Maple-flavoured syrup or pancake syrup are not adequate substitutes for the real thing.

MARSALA a sweet, fortified wine to which additional alcohol has been added, most commonly in the form of brandy.

MAYONNAISE we use whole-egg mayonnaise in our recipes unless indicated otherwise.

MILK, SWEETENED CONDENSED a canned milk product consisting of milk with more than half the water removed and sugar added to the remaining milk.

MIXED SPICE a classic spice mixture generally containing caraway, allspice, coriander, cumin, nutmeg and ginger, although cinnamon and other spices can be added.

MUSHROOMS
button small, cultivated white mushrooms with a mild flavour. If the mushrooms are unspecified, use button mushrooms.
flat large, flat mushrooms with a rich earthy flavour, ideal for filling and barbecuing. They are sometimes misnamed field mushrooms, which are wild mushrooms.
oyster also known as abalone; grey-white mushrooms shaped like a fan. Prized for their smooth texture and subtle, oyster-like flavour.
portobello mature, fully open swiss brown mushrooms; larger in size and more robust in flavour.
swiss brown also known as roman or cremini. Brown mushrooms with a full-bodied flavour.

MUSLIN inexpensive, undyed, finely woven cotton fabric used in cooking to strain stocks and sauces; if unavailable, use disposable coffee filter papers.

MUSTARD
dijon also called french mustard. Pale brown, creamy, distinctively flavoured, mild french mustard.
powder finely ground white (yellow) mustard seeds.
wholegrain also called seeded. A french-style coarse-grain mustard made from crushed mustard seeds and dijon-style french mustard.

NUTMEG a strong and pungent spice ground from the dried nut of an evergreen tree native to Indonesia. Usually found ground, but the flavour is more intense from a whole nut, available from spice shops, so it's best to grate your own.

OIL
cooking spray we use a cholesterol-free cooking spray made from canola oil.
olive made from ripened olives. Extra virgin and virgin are the first and second press, respectively, of the olives and are therefore considered the best; 'light' refers to taste, not fat levels.
vegetable oils sourced from plants rather than animal fats.

ONIONS
baby larger than shallots; pickled in brine or cooked in stews and casseroles.
brown and white are interchangeable, however white onions have a more pungent flesh.
green (scallions) also called, incorrectly, shallot; an immature onion picked before the bulb has formed, with a long, green edible stalk.
pickling also known as cocktail or baby onions; are baby brown onions that are larger than shallots.
red also known as spanish, red spanish or bermuda onion; a sweet-flavoured, large, purple-red onion.
shallots also called french shallots, golden shallots or eschalots; small brown-skinned elongated members of the onion family.

PAPRIKA ground, dried red capsicum (bell pepper); there are many types available, including sweet, hot, mild and smoked.

PASTRY
fillo fragile, paper-thin sheets of pastry; brush each sheet with oil or melted butter, stack in layers, then cut and fold as directed.
puff a crisp, light pastry; layers of dough and fat (margarine or butter) are folded and rolled many times making many layers. When baked, it becomes a high, crisp, flaky pastry.
sheets ready-rolled packaged sheets of frozen puff and shortcrust pastry, available from supermarkets.

PEARL BARLEY a nutritious grain used in soups and stews. Pearl barley has had the husk removed, then been steamed and polished so that only the 'pearl' of the original grain remains.

PEAR, BEURRE BOSC this firm and crunchy pear is the best choice for cooking because it holds its shape.

PEAR CIDER, or perry as it may be known in the UK, is a fermented cider made from pear juice. World-wide it is not as well-known as apple cider, but it has been around for centuries. While commercially-produced pear cider may be referred to as perry, there is some argument against this by some professional liquour organisations who believe perry can only be associated with a cider that is traditionally made.

PEPITAS are the pale green kernels of dried pumpkin seeds; they can be bought plain or salted. We use plain unsalted pepitas in our recipes.

PEPPERCORNS
black the most common type is the black peppercorn, which is picked when the berry is not quite ripe, then dried until it shrivels and the skin turns dark brown to black. It is slightly hot with a hint of sweetness.
green the soft, under-ripe berry of the pepper vine; is most commonly sold pickled in brine or vinegar, or freeze-dried. It has a fresh flavour that's less pungent than the berry in its other forms. Find them in some larger supermarkets and most Asian grocery stores.

PINE NUTS also called pignoli.

POLENTA also known as cornmeal; a flour-like cereal made of dried corn (maize) sold ground in several textures; also the name of the dish made from it.

PORK
cutlets cut from the ribs.
fillet skinless, boneless eye-fillet cut from the loin.
ham hock the lower portion of the leg; includes the meat, fat and bone. Most have been cured, smoked or both.
loin runs across the back of the pig.
rack joined row of trimmed cutlets.
shoulder joint; bone may be in or out.

RAISINS dried sweet grapes.

ROLLED OATS oat groats (oats that have been husked) steam-softened, flattened with rollers, dried and packaged for consumption as a cereal product.

SAUSAGES seasoned and spiced minced (ground) meat mixed with cereal and packed into casings. Also known as snags or bangers.

STERILISING JARS it's important the jars be as clean as possible; make sure your hands, the preparation area, tea towels and cloths etc, are clean, too. The aim is to finish sterilising the jars and lids at the same time the preserve is ready to be bottled; the hot preserve should be bottled into hot, dry clean jars. Jars that aren't sterilised properly can cause deterioration of the preserves during storage. Always start with cleaned washed jars and lids, then follow one of these methods:
(1) Put the jars and lids through the hottest cycle of a dishwasher without using any detergent, or
(2) Lie the jars down in a boiler with the lids, cover them with cold water then cover the boiler with a lid. Bring the water to the boil over a high heat and boil the jars for 20 minutes, or
(3) Stand the jars upright, without touching each other, on a wooden board on the lowest shelf in the oven. Turn the oven to the lowest possible temperature, close the oven door and leave the jars to heat through for 30 minutes.
Next, remove the jars from the oven or dishwasher with a towel, or from the boiling water with tongs and rubber-gloved hands; the water will evaporate from hot wet jars quite quickly. Stand the jars upright and not touching each other on a wooden board, or a bench covered with a clean towel, to protect and insulate the bench. Fill the jars as directed in the recipe; secure the lids tightly, holding jars firmly with a towel or an oven mitt. Leave preserves at room temperature to cool before storing.

SUGAR
brown a very soft, finely granulated sugar that retains molasses for its colour and flavour.
caster (superfine) finely granulated table sugar.
dark brown a moist, dark brown sugar with a rich, distinctive full flavour from molasses syrup.
demerara small-grained golden-coloured crystal sugar.
icing (confectioners') also known as powdered sugar; pulverised granulated sugar crushed together with a small amount of cornflour (cornstarch).
raw natural brown granulated sugar.
white (granulated) coarse, granulated table sugar, also known as crystal sugar.

SULTANAS dried grapes, also known as golden raisins.

TARTARIC ACID a natural food acid found in many plants especially grapes. Helps to preserve and set foods, and is also an ingredient in cream of tartar, so may be found in some baking powders.

THYME a member of the mint family; there are many types of this herb but the one we use most, simply called thyme in most shops, is french thyme; it has tiny grey-green leaves that give off a pungent minty, light-lemon aroma.
lemon thyme a herb with a lemony scent (due to the high level of citral oil in its leaves – an oil also found in lemon, orange, verbena and lemon grass). The scent is enhanced by crushing the leaves in your hands before using the herb.

TOMATOES
paste triple-concentrated tomato puree used to flavour soups, stews and sauces.
semi-dried partially dried tomato pieces in olive oil; softer and juicier than sun-dried, these are not a preserve so do not keep as long as sun-dried.
sun-dried tomato pieces dried with salt; this dehydrates the tomato and concentrates the flavour. We use sun-dried tomatoes packaged in oil, unless stated otherwise.

TREACLE thick, dark syrup not unlike molasses; a by-product of sugar refining.

VANILLA
bean dried, long, thin pod from a tropical golden orchid; the tiny black seeds impart a luscious flavour.
extract vanilla beans that have been submerged in alcohol. Vanilla essence is not a suitable substitute.

VEAL SCHNITZELS (escalopes) thinly sliced steak available crumbed or plain; we use plain schnitzel in our recipes.

VERJUICE from the french 'vert jus' or 'verjus' meaning, 'green juice'. It is the unfermented, slightly acidic juice of semi-ripe red and white wine grapes.

VINEGAR
balsamic originally from Modena, Italy. Made from the juice of trebbiano grapes; it is a deep rich brown colour with a sweet and sour flavour.
cider (apple cider) made from fermented apples.
brown malt made from fermented malt and beech shavings.
rice a colourless vinegar made from fermented rice and flavoured with sugar and salt. Sherry can be substituted.
white wine made from a blend of white wines.

WORCESTERSHIRE SAUCE thin, dark-brown spicy sauce used as a seasoning for meat, gravies and cocktails, and as a condiment.

YEAST (dried and fresh) a raising agent used in dough making. Granular (7g sachets) and fresh compressed (20g blocks) yeast can almost always be substituted for the other when yeast is called for.

YOGHURT we use plain full-cream yoghurt in our recipes.
Greek-style plain yoghurt strained in a cloth (muslin) to remove the whey and to give it a creamy consistency.

INDEX

Published in 2013 by Bauer Media Books
Bauer Media Books is a division of Bauer Media Limited.
54 Park St, Sydney
GPO Box 4088, Sydney, NSW 2001.
phone (02) 9282 8618; fax (02) 9126 3702
www.awwcookbooks.com.au

MEDIA GROUP
BAUER MEDIA BOOKS

Publishing Director - Gerry Reynolds
Publisher - Sally Wright
Editorial and Food Director - Pamela Clark
Sales and Rights Director - Brian Cearnes
Creative Director - Hieu Chi Nguyen

Published and Distributed in the United Kingdom by Octopus Publishing Group
Endeavour House
189 Shaftesbury Avenue
London WC2H 8JY
United Kingdom
phone (+44)(0)207 632 5400; fax (+44)(0)207 632 5405
info@octopus-publishing.co.uk
www.octopusbooks.co.uk

Printed by Toppan Printing Co., China

International foreign language rights, Brian Cearnes, Bauer Media Books bcearnes@bauer-media.com.au

A catalogue record for this book is available from the British Library.
ISBN: 978 174245 375 0 (pbk.)
© Bauer Media Ltd 2013
ABN 18 053 273 546

THE AUSTRALIAN Women's Weekly

ALSO FROM THE BEST-SELLING COOKERY SERIES OF ALL TIME

Delicious winter favourites creamy turkey stew with mustard p50 lamb shank, fennel and vegetable soup p8 borscht p11 pork and fennel soup p16 best-ever bolognese sauce p38 chicken cacciatore p39 coq au vin p44 chinese chicken hot pot p48 osso buco with mixed mushrooms p56 portuguese-style chicken p77 greek-style roast lamb with potatoes p81 red curry lamb shanks p84 mandarin and almond pudding p112

Treat yourself with orange almond victoria sponge p104 neenish & pineapple tarts p37 custard fruit flans p38 cucumber sandwiches p6 vanilla bean scones p17 chocolate éclairs p30 cherry bakewell tarts p42 rhubarb frangipane tarts p46 portuguese custard tarts p50 madeleines p56 chocolate french macaroons p63 rosewater meringues p68 jelly cakes p96 raspberry cream sponge p108 mixed berry hazelnut cake p111

Some of the recipes in this book: almond butter cake; angel food cake; banana caramel layer cake; carrot cake with lemon cream cheese frosting; celebration fruit cake; chocolate coconut squares; devil's food cake; mississippi mud cake; opera gateau; sacher torte; cinnamon teacake; cut & keep butter cake; featherlight sponge cake

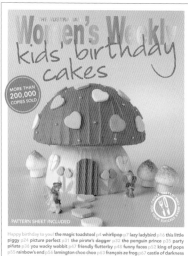

Happy birthday to you! the magic toadstool p4 whirlipop p7 lazy ladybird p16 this little piggy p24 picture perfect p31 the pirate's dagger p32 the penguin prince p35 party piñata p36 you wacky wabbit p47 friendly flutterby p48 funny faces p52 king of pops p55 rainbow's end p56 lamington choo choo p63 françois ze frog p67 castle of darkness p68 sam the tool man p71 girlie ghost p76 one p92 three p96 seven p104 nine p108

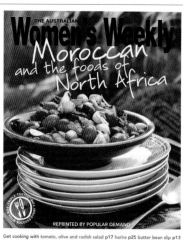

Get cooking with tomato, olive and radish salad p17 harira p25 butter bean dip p13 beetroot, fennel and lentil salad p14 tuna salad p30 grilled eggplant with tabbouleh p36 fried zucchini p40 roasted pumpkin couscous p44 pumpkin and split pea tagine p48 chicken with couscous stuffing p57 harissa marinated lamb p62 kofta p66 za'atar lamb p70 beef and prune tagine p76 poached nectarines p103 semolina slice p108